ENGLISH G

| Baden-Württemberg |

access 2

WORKBOOK

Vokabel Trainer

Cornelsen

Vokabeltrainer-App

Verfügbar für: iOS, Android und Windows Phone

scook

AUDIOS online

Deine **interaktiven Gratis-Übungen** und **Audios** findest du auf scook.de. Dort gibst du den unten stehenden Zugangscode in die Box ein.

Dein Zugangscode auf www.scook.de

Die Gratis-Übungen und Audios können dort nach Bestätigung der AGB und Lizenzbedingungen genutzt werden.

68xaw-3yzjt

Cornelsen

In the holidays

Die interaktive Übung 1 findest du auf www.scook.de. Zum Einloggen auf Scook brauchst du den Code auf Seite 1.

1 Holiday talk ➜ *SB (pp. 8–9)*

a) ○ The Plymouth kids talk about their holidays. Match the photos and the speech bubbles.

Justin

Sam

Lucy

Abby

Hot sun and beautiful blue water! It's fantastic for sailing. I loved the beach.

We had a great time with the animals on the farm – and I can make scones now.

I saw lots of places with Dad. Camping is really exciting – but it can be scary too! You don't see bears when you go camping on Dartmoor!

Dad and I had fun in the sea with the big waves. Caravans are fun too.

b) ○ Put in: was, wasn't, were, weren't.

Lots of crabs were on holiday in Plymouth Sound – so I was happy! Yummy!

1 Sam wasn't in the mountains. He ________ by the sea.

2 Sam and his family ________ in a caravan. They ________ in a holiday flat.

3 Justin ________ in Plymouth, UK. He ________ in Plymouth, Massachusetts.

4 Lucy and Maya ________ at home all the time. They ________ on Dartmoor.

5 Abby ________ in Rome. The Blackwells ________ on holiday in Turkey.

c) ● Write two sentences in the simple past about the students' holidays. You can use words from the box.

caravan · Eden Project · camping · mountains · plants · rainforest · scones · the sea · visit · weather

1 Justin was in the USA. He visited ________________

____

2 Abby ________________________________

____

3 Sam ________________________________

____

4 Lucy and Maya ________________________________

____

____

2 WORDS The weather ➜ SB (p. 11)

a) ○ Write the weather words.

We went to Rome. The weather was too h o t for me. After our visit to Rome we had a holiday flat by the sea. It was great there, w _ _ _ and _ _ _ _ _ _. And you?

We had a caravan near a lake in Germany. We went walking in the mountains, but it was _ _ _ d and _ _ _ d _. Some days were _ l _ _ _ _ and _ _ _ _ _ _ too, so we got w _ _. But the last day of the holiday was _ _ _ and sunny – of course!

b) Finish the sentences. Use two or three weather words in each sentence.

1 It's good weather for a day at the beach when it's ______________________

2 The best weather for sailing is when ______________________

3 Swimming at the Lido is no fun when ______________________

3 REVISION Find the verbs (Simple past: regular verbs) ➜ SB (p. 11) • GF 1 (p. 88)

○ 02 (Circle) the verbs in the snake and write them in the simple past. Use your exercise book. Say the simple past forms. Then listen and check.

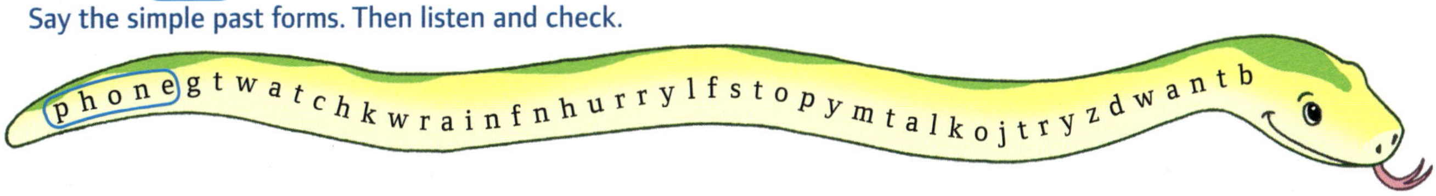

4 REVISION Justin saw a bear (Simple past: irregular verbs) ➜ SB (p. 11) • GF 1 (p. 88)

○ (Circle) and write six irregular simple past forms. Then use the forms to finish the sentences.

s	s	s	f	e	d	g	h
a	s	e	n	t	k	o	a
w	e	n	t	n	f	t	d

→ ______ ______ ______

↓ ______ ______ ______

1 Justin never goes camping with his mum, but in the USA he ____________ camping with his dad.

2 Justin never sees bears in Plymstock, but in the USA he ____________ a big black bear.

3 Sam never sends pictures from Plymouth, but he ____________ Justin a picture from Weston-super-Mare.

4 Sam usually gets up early, but in Weston-super-Mare he ____________ up late.

5 At home Sam has go-kart races with his friends. On holiday he ____________ a go-kart race with his dad.

6 Lucy's grandpa feeds the farm animals, but in the holidays Lucy and Maya ____________ them too.

5 WORDS What goes together? ➜ SB (p. 11)

a) ○ What goes together? Match the words and write them down.

do	fun/an ice cream	play	a museum/friends
go	text messages	take	football/computer games
have	new friends/a video	visit	postcards/emails
make	swimming/shopping	watch	photos
send	sports	write	TV/ DVDs

do sports,

b) ● Imagine you were on holiday in Turkey, like Abby. Write an email to an English cousin in your exercise book. Tell him/her what you did there. Use weather words and ideas from part a).

Hi, ...!
This year we went on holiday to Turkey. It was great! The weather was ... so I/we ... One day I/we ...

6 At home in the holidays ➜ SB (p. 11)

a) ○ Collect ideas in a mind map about what you can do at home in the holidays.
Use your exercise book. Words from exercises 3–5 and the ideas in the box can help you:

cinema · games · garden · hobbies · inside · outside · places · sports · shopping mall · swimming pool · people · zoo

b) ● Use your mind map to tell a partner what you and your family did at home in the holidays. Use the simple past.

Holidays at home are good too. In the last week of the holidays the weather was warm and sunny, so I/we ...

7 REVISION They didn't do that (Simple past: statements) ➜ SB (p. 11) • GF 1 (p. 88)

What's wrong? Write two correct sentences.

TIP: Look at pp. 8–9 in your student's book again.

1 Abby went to Germany with her family. *She didn't go to Germany. She went to Turkey.*

2 Justin went to New York.

3 Lucy and Maya visited Maya's uncle.

4 The Bennetts had a holiday flat.

5 Abby met a nice boy from Germany.

8 REVISION Justin's questions (Simple past: *yes/no* questions) ➜ *SB (p. 11) • GF 1 (p. 88)*

a) Justin asked Lucy about the holidays. Finish Justin's questions and Lucy's short answers.

Justin	Lucy
1 *Did you go* (you/go) to your grandparents' farm?	Yes, *I did.* It isn't far from Plymouth.
2 ______ (Holly/go) with you?	No, ______ She stayed at home.
3 ______ (you/have) good weather?	______ It was cold and windy.
4 ______ (Abby/like) Turkey?	______ She said it was great.
5 ______ (it/rain) in Turkey?	______ It was hot and sunny.
6 ______ (Abby/do) lots of sport?	______ She went sailing every day.

b) Write questions for your partner about his/her holidays. Use Did ... and the words in brackets ( ). Ask your partner the questions in class.

1 (camping) ______

2 (holiday flat) ______

3 (family) ______

4 (new friends) ______

5 (cinema) ______

6 (sports) ______

9 Sorry? (Simple past: *wh*-questions) ➜ *SB (p. 12) • GF 1 (p. 88)*

An English friend phones to tell you about his/her holidays. You don't understand some words, so you ask questions. Write your questions with what, where, when, why and how …

Your friend	YOU
1 We went to **Scotland** in the holidays.	Sorry, where *did you go?*
2 We went **to visit my uncle**.	Sorry, ______
3 We went **by car**.	Sorry, ______
4 We visited **some great castles**.	Sorry, ______
5 One day we went **to Edinburgh**.	______
6 We saw **some beautiful lakes**.	______
7 We came back **yesterday**.	______

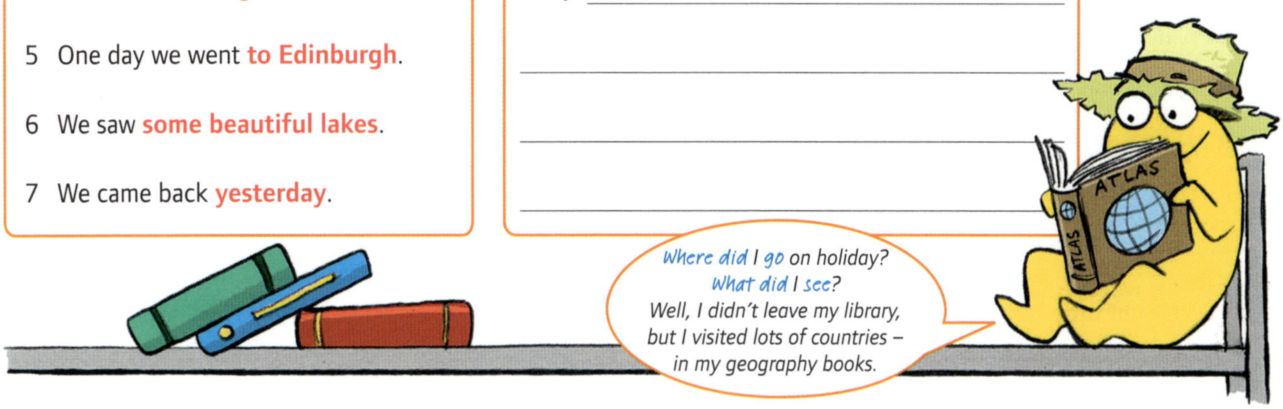

10 Where did you go? ➔ SB (p. 12) • SF 15 (p. 87)

● 03 First listen to Amira and Nick. Then answer Amira's questions about your holidays. Press the pause button[1].

...

Amira: Hi! Did you have a good holiday?
You: *Yes, thanks. It was great. I/We ...*
Amira: Did you go away or did you stay at home?
You: *We ...*

11 WORDS Phone words ➔ SB (p. 12)

a) ○ What goes together? Match the words.

leave	the phone
hold	back
answer	to (someone)
phone	a message
be	on (a minute)
speak	in/out

b) Write the sentences in English.

1 Kann ich bitte mit Lucy sprechen? ______

2 Bleib bitte dran. ______

3 Kannst du später zurückrufen? ______

4 Möchtest du eine Nachricht hinterlassen? ______

c) ● With a partner, write a phone call and present it to the class. Use words from a) and b).

12 Two phone calls ➔ SB (p. 12) • SF 14 (pp. 86–87)

a) 04 Listen to two phone calls. Circle the correct sentences. You need the letters in part b).

In the first call:

1 a) Pippa answers the phone. **Y**
b) Nina answers the phone. **D**
2 a) Nina is listening to music. **A**
b) Nina is out. **D**
3 a) Nina is shopping with her mum. **A**
b) Nina is shopping with her friends. **R**
4 a) Dan leaves a message. **R**
b) Pippa tells Dan to phone back. **K**

In the second call:

5 a) Nina calls Dan. **B**
b) Dan calls Nina. **I**
6 a) Nina went to a café with her mum. **C**
b) Nina went for an ice cream with her friends. **O**
7 a) Nina's family visited a cousin in New York. **R**
b) Nina's family visited friends in New York. **W**
8 a) Nina asks Dan to her house. **A**
b) Dan asks Nina to his house. **S**

b) In the right order, the letters after the correct answers tell you where Nina was.

➔ She was at the _ _ _ _ _ _ _ _ .

[1] Press the pause button. [pres ðə ˈpɔːz ˌbʌtn] *Drück die Pausetaste.*

13 STUDY SKILLS Making notes with a crib sheet ➔ SB (p. 13) • SF 5 (p. 85)

a) Read Lucy's information about the Eden Project.

Welcome to The Eden Project

The Eden Project is an exciting place.
It has flowers[1] and plants from hot countries.
It even has a real tropical rainforest.

The rainforest is in a dome. You go inside the dome and it's really hot, between 30 and 40 degrees. You can see how sugar[2] grows and where chocolate comes from. You can see papaya and banana trees, and lemon[3] and olive trees in the Mediterranean[4] Dome.

Outside the domes there are beautiful gardens with flowers and trees, and they grow fruit and vegetables too.

There's a nice restaurant with great pizzas, salads and ice cream. There's a shop with books, postcards, toys and games too.

The Eden Project is in Cornwall.
It's just one hour by train[5] from Plymouth.
Then you can take a bus.

It's open every day from 10 am to 6 pm.
In summer it's sometimes open till 8 pm.

b) Make a crib sheet to help you remember interesting or important things. Use notes and symbols/small pictures.
Ideas for symbols: flowers, plants, dome, chocolate, banana, trees, fruit, pizza, train, bus …

c) ● Make a crib sheet about an interesting place or sight in your town or village.
Then use your crib sheet and tell a partner eight sentences about it.

14 REVISION Right or wrong? (Simple present: statements) ➔ SB (p. 16) • GF 2 (pp. 88–89)

Finish the sentences with simple present forms. Find and correct the wrong sentences.

TIP: Look at p. 15 in your student's book again.

1 Lucy's mum often *makes* (make) plans for her. ✓ ______
2 Sam's mum often *makes* (make) plans for him. ✗ *She doesn't make plans for him.*
3 Sam ______ (watch) TV in the afternoon. ◯ ______
4 Lucy ______ (know) Leo. ◯ ______
5 Sam ______ (have to) look after Lily. ◯ ______
6 Leo ______ (be) in Year 7. ◯ ______
7 Leo and Sam ______ (go) to different schools. ◯ ______
8 Leo, Lucy and Sam ______ (play) football. ◯ ______

[1]flower ['flaʊə] *Blume* [2]sugar ['ʃʊɡə] *Zucker* [3]lemon ['lemən] *Zitrone* [4]Mediterranean [ˌmedɪtə'reɪniən] *Mittelmeer* [5]train [treɪn] *Zug*

15 REVISION The Plymouth kids (Simple present: questions) ➜ SB (p. 16) • GF 2 (pp. 88–89)

a) Write questions with Do/Does or with a question word + do/does.

1 Leo/to Plymstock/to Coombe Dean/go? *Does Leo go to Plymstock or to Coombe Dean?*

2 Leo/where/live? ______

3 play/Sam and Justin/basketball/volleyball? ______

4 Sam/do/what? ______

5 the first lesson/9 o'clock/9.15/start? ______

6 go/Abby and Maya/sailing/skating? ______

b) ● With a partner, take turns to ask and answer the questions in a).

16 Ask in English, please! ➜ SB (p. 16) • SF 12 (p. 86)

Sam from Plymouth is visiting you in the holidays.
On the first morning your mum and your 8-year-old brother ask Sam lots of questions, in German. Ask Sam the questions in English.

TIP: Don't translate[1]!
Leave out[2] what is not important.

Mum: Frag Sam, was er zum Frühstück isst. Mag er vielleicht einen Joghurt?

You: *What do you eat/have for breakfast, Sam? Do you like yoghurt?*

Mum: Frag ihn, wann die Schule in Plymouth anfängt. Muss er auch so früh aufstehen wie ihr?

You: ______

Mum: Frag ihn, wie er in die Schule kommt. Mit dem Bus? Oder zu Fuß?

You: ______

Mum: Frag ihn, ob seine kleine Schwester auch schon in die Schule geht.

You: ______

Brother: Sam hat dir erzählt, dass er Kung Fu lernt. Warum gerade das? Es ist ziemlich schwer, denke ich.

You: ______

Brother: Frag ihn auch, ob er Fußball spielt. Vielleicht kann er am Nachmittag mit uns im Park spielen.

You: ______

Brother: Mag er Mathe? Vielleicht kann er mir ein paar Tipps geben.

You: ______

TIP: Use only words you know.
For 'ein paar Tipps geben' you can say *help*.

Mum: Frag ihn, wie es ihm bei uns in Deutschland gefällt.

You: ______

Sam: It's very nice. I like it here – but people ask lots of questions!

[1]translate [træns'leɪt] *übersetzen* [2]leave out [liːv aʊt] *auslassen*

17 REVISION Who did what? (Simple past: questions with *who*) ➜ *SB (p. 17) • GF 1 (p. 88)*

a) Write questions with Who …? and verbs in the simple past.

Who

1 have · 2 go · 3 feed · 4 see · 5 make · 6 meet · 7 visit · 8 move

to Turkey · animals on a farm · the Eden Project · a bear · a caravan by the sea · a nice German girl · scones · into number 37

1 *Who had a caravan by the sea?* ____________ 5 ____________

2 ____________ 6 ____________

3 ____________ 7 ____________

4 ____________ 8 ____________

b) EXTRA Ask the questions in class. Someone has to answer.

18 Who phoned who? (Subject/Object questions) ➜ *SB (p. 17) • GF 3 (p. 89–90)*

a) Yesterday the friends made lots of phone calls. Who phoned who? Write the answers and questions.

1 Who phoned Nina? – *Emily*

2 Who did Nina phone? – *Charlotte*

3 Who did Charlotte phone? – ____________

4 Who phoned Dan? – ____________

5 ____________ – Nina

6 ____________ – Nick

b) Write two questions each with Who …? Then write the answers. Ask about …

1 Emily: *Who phoned Emily?* – *Charlotte*

Who did ____________ – ____________

2 Amira: ____________ – ____________

____________ – ____________

3 Nick: ____________ – ____________

____________ – ____________

c) Answer the questions. Write full sentences.

1 Who phones or texts you every day/week? ____________

2 Who do you phone or text every day/week? ____________

19 WORDS Getting in touch ➔ SB (p. 18)

a) ○ Write the missing words in the puzzle and find the word in the blue boxes.

1 I usually write …, not letters.

2 I always send my friends … from my holidays.

3 When I'm on holiday, I write in my … every day.

4 Facebook is a social networking …

5 How many phone … do you make every day?

6 My sister sends lots of text … every evening.

➔ The word is: _ _ _ _ _ _ .

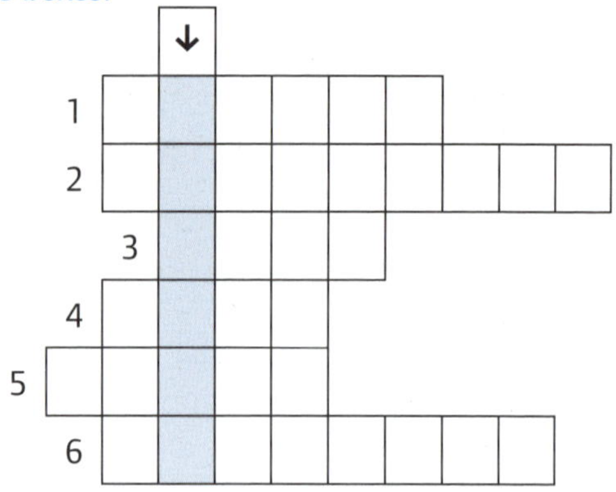

b) How do you get in touch or stay in touch with your friends? Finish the sentences.

On school days I ______________________________

In the school holidays I ______________________________

20 Youth hostel[1] rules ➔ SB (p. 18) • SF 12 (p. 86)

You are at a youth hostel in Germany with your class. There are some English kids there too. They ask you some questions about the rules. Answer them in English in your exercise book.

TIP:
man darf:
you can,
you're allowed to …
man darf nicht:
you can't,
you aren't allowed to …
man muss:
you have to

Willkommen in unserer Jugendherberge!

- Bitte die Schlaf- und Aufenthaltsräume sauber halten.
- Es ist nicht erlaubt, in den Schlafräumen zu essen. Frühstück, Mittag- und Abendessen werden im Speisesaal serviert.
- Bitte während der Nachtruhe (22–7 Uhr) in den Schlafräumen die Handys ausschalten.
- Laute Musik sowie störendes Verhalten auf den Gängen ist untersagt.
- Gäste werden gebeten, die Schlafräume bis 10 Uhr zu räumen.

- Der Spielplatz und die Tischtennisplatten dürfen bis 21 Uhr benutzt werden.
- Die Aufenthaltsräume (mit TV, DVD-Player und Internet) stehen den Gästen bis 23 Uhr zur Verfügung.

1 Where can we get something to eat?

2 Are we allowed to eat and drink in the bedrooms?

3 Can I use my mobile at night?

4 Are we allowed to watch TV?

5 Can we play table tennis in the garden?

6 What time do we have to leave tomorrow?

1 You can get something to eat in the dining room.

[1] youth hostel ['ju:θ hɒstl] *Jugendherberge*

21 READING COURSE Understanding new words

➔ SB (p. 19) • SF6 (p. 85)

a) ○ Read the text and try to understand the underlined new words without a dictionary.

When you walk on Dartmoor, you can't miss the famous Dartmoor ponies. Everybody knows them. The pony is the Park's logo. They always live on the moor, in summer and in winter. You often see them together in small herds. Dartmoor ponies have owners, usually farmers from the region, so they aren't truly wild. The ponies often have ear tags, so their owners can identify them. The ponies can be brown, grey or black. Their heads are small, but their legs are strong. They're good jumpers.

Foals are usually born from May to August. Everybody loves these beautiful young horses. Dartmoor ponies are very popular animals. But be careful. Don't stroke or feed them on the moor. They're usually friendly, but they can bite. Farmers sometimes take ponies to market to sell them for riding. Many children would like to have their own pony at home as a pet. But ponies aren't like dogs and cats. You need more than a big garden. The moor is their real home.

b) What helps you to understand the new words? Write the underlined words in the lists.

The words around it help you to guess	The picture	Other words with the same meaning	You know part of the word	You know a similar word in German	A similar word in another language
famous					fameux (Fr.)

22 EXTRA Background file: Boarding schools

➔ SB (p. 21)

a) Are the statements about British boarding schools right or wrong? (Circle) a letter.

		Right	Wrong
1	There are more than a hundred thousand students at British boarding schools.	R	S
2	Students at boarding schools go home at the weekend.	O	W
3	Parents of boarding school students often went to the same school.	R	G
4	Only British students go to boarding schools in England.	W	O
5	Most boarding schools are private.	G	T
6	Some boarding schools are very expensive.	T	A
7	You don't have to pay to go to Eton College.	H	A
8	Eton College is a school for boys.	H	O

b) In the right order, the letters for the correct answers tell you where a famous person went to school:

➔ _ _ _ _ _ _ _ _ .

c) ● Think of two things you like/you don't like about boarding schools. Write four sentences in your exercise book.

23 REVISION The Blackwells (Present progressive: positive statements) ➜ SB (p. 22) • GF 4 (p. 90)

a) What are the Blackwells doing? Finish the sentences. Use verbs in the present progressive.

1  2  3  4  5  6 

1 On Sundays, Mr Blackwell often works in the garden, *but today he's reading his newspapers.*

2 In the afternoon, Mrs Blackwell sometimes sits in the garden, but today ______

3 Tim often rides his bike with his friends, but today ______

4 On Sundays, the Blackwells often play games on the beach, but just now ______

5 After tea, Skip usually goes for a walk, but at the moment ______

6 In the evening, Mr and Mrs Blackwell often go running in the park, but now ______

b) Why do you think they are doing different things today? Write a sentence.

Maybe ______

c) Write five sentences like in a) about you and your family. Use your exercise book.

24 What are they doing next Saturday? (Present progressive: future meaning) ➜ SB (p. 22) • GF 4 (p. 90)

a) Correct the statements 1–4.

1 

2 

3 

4 

1 Sam is going shopping next Saturday. *He isn't going shopping next Saturday. He's playing basketball.*

2 Lucy and Holly are visiting an aunt next Saturday. ______

______

3 Justin is filming on Saturday afternoon. ______

4 Abby is buying a new bike next Saturday. ______

______

b) What are you doing next Saturday morning, afternoon and evening? Write three sentences in your exercise book.

On Saturday morning I'm helping Mum/Dad ...

25 TEXT My USA logbook ➜ SB (pp. 24–25)

a) Read pp. 24–25 of your student's book again. Find and write the missing words from the story.

1 The US word for 'flat' is …
2 Justin helped his dad in the kitchen. He washed the …
3 At Rosie's Diner Justin ordered six …
4 Their … was next to a small river.
5 Justin helped his dad with the …
6 They made marshmallows on the open …
7 When Justin woke up, his dad was … next to him.
8 When Justin turned on his …, he saw a black bear.

In the right order, the letters in the blue boxes tell you the name of a place Justin visited on his trip:

➜ Mt. _ _ _ _ _ _ _ _ _

b) ● Which days of Justin's holiday do the pictures show? How do you know? Write the day or date and one or two sentences for each picture.

1 

2 

3 

4 

Picture 1: It's Justin's first day in Boston. Justin is helping his dad in the kitchen./ Justin is washing the dishes.

Picture 2: It's

Picture 3:

Picture 4:

c) ● Which part of Justin's trip do you think was really interesting or exciting? Say why. Write a short paragraph with six or more sentences in your exercise book.

A school day

1 WORDS Good morning! ➜ SB (pp. 28–29)

Finish the sentences.

1 At the Bennetts' house the doorbell ______________, but Sam doesn't hear it.

2 Before Miss Bell arrives, students ______________ outside the classroom.

3 At registration, Miss Bell ______________ which students are at school.

4 Miss Bell ______________________________ of all the students in the class.

5 There are ______________ for singers and ______________ for the school show.

6 ______________________ musical is *We Will Rock You*.

2 What are they going to do today? (*going to*-future) ➜ SB (p. 31) • GF5 (p. 90)

Finish the sentences.

1 After school, Holly *is going to play tennis.*

2 After school, Sam ______________________________

3 In the lunch break, Lucy and Leo ______________________________

4 In the evening, Maya ______________________________

5 After homework, Justin ______________________________

6 After dinner, Lucy and Holly ______________________________

3 In the break (*going to*-future: mixed forms) ➜ *SB (p. 31) • GF 5 (p. 90)*

be · dance · join (3x) · sing (2x) · start · ~~stay~~ · watch

a) Finish Sam and Justin's dialogue with forms of *be going to* and the correct verbs.

Sam: I'*m going to stay* in the Basketball Club this year. And you ________________ too, right?

Justin: Right. And the others? ________ they ________________ basketball too?

Sam: Well, no. Lucy and Leo ________________ the School Show Club.

Lucy ________________ a song at the auditions for the musical,

and Leo ________________ .

Justin: Hmm … So they ________________ our team.

________ you ________________ in the musical too?

Sam: Me? Oh, no! That isn't for me. I ________________ at the auditions.

Justin: But Lucy and Leo are good. I ________________ them. Why don't you come too?

Sam: Erm, OK. Maybe they need someone for kung fu in the musical! What do you think?

**b) What are you going to do this school year? Are you going to join a club?
Write two or more sentences in your exercise book.**

4 A phone call ➜ *SB (p. 31) • SF 14 (pp. 86–87)*

a) ○ 05 Listen to Nina and Dan. Then tick (✓) the correct box.

They talk about: 1 friends and family. ▢ 2 the new school year. ▢ 3 sports and hobbies. ▢

b) Read the following statements, then listen again. Are the statements right or wrong? Circle a letter.

	Right	Wrong
1 There are two new students in Nina's class: a girl from Germany and a boy from London.	T	L
2 Nina is going to learn German this year.	E	R
3 Last year Nina was in three clubs.	A	P
4 She isn't going to stay in the Tennis Club.	L	A
5 Nina thinks that musicals are interesting.	S	M
6 Dan says auditions for the Plymstock musical are going to be on Tuesday.	I	B
7 Coombe Dean did a musical last year.	T	N
8 Dan would like to be in the Plymstock musical.	A	B
9 Dan plays an instrument.	L	S
10 Dan is going to stay in two clubs.	O	K

c) In the correct order, the letters for the correct answers give you the name of Dan's favourite school club:

➜ the _ _ _ _ _ _ _ _ _ _ Club.

5 Which is faster? (Comparison of adjectives) ➜ SB (p. 34) • GF6 (p. 91)

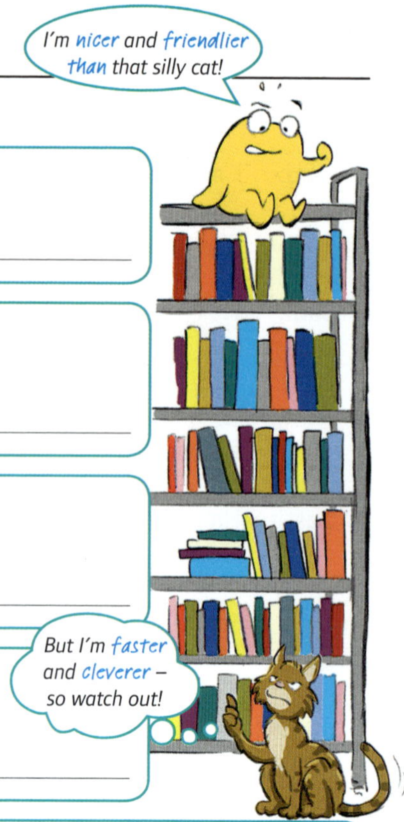

Compare the pictures. What do you think? Write sentences with … than …

1 

fast:

I think a giraffe is faster than an elephant.

2 

easy:

____

3 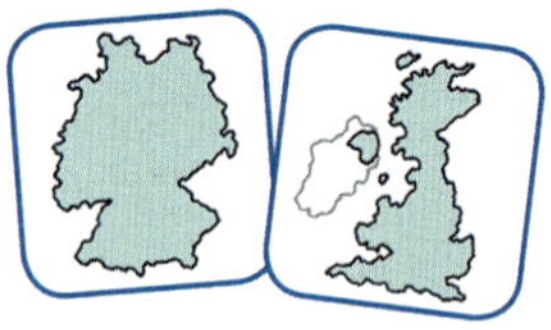

big:

____

4 

nice:

____

5 

scary:

____

6 Look at the map, Sam! (Comparison of adjectives: mixed forms) ➜ SB (p. 34) • GF6 (p. 91)

a) ● Sam and Lucy are doing geography homework together. Finish their dialogue with comparisons.

Sam: Which is the *biggest* (big) country, England, Scotland or Wales? Oh, silly question. Sorry.

It's England, of course. I mean, is Scotland ________ ________ (big) Wales?

Lucy: Yes, it is. Look at the map, Sam! And the ________ (large) lakes are in Scotland.

Sam: Right, Lucy. I know that. But is Loch Ness ________ ________ ________ (large) Loch Lomond?

Lucy: No, it isn't. Loch Ness is a bit ________ ________ (small) Loch Lomond. Look at the map, Sam!

Sam: OK, but England has the ________ (long) river, right? It's the Thames[1].

Lucy: No, it isn't the Thames, Sam. The Thames isn't ________ ________ ________ (long) the Severn. Look …

Sam: I know, Lucy: 'Look at the map, Sam'. And what about the ________ (high) mountain?

Ben Nevis is in Scotland and Snowdon is in Wales, right? Ben Nevis is 1344 m high.

Lucy: Oh, really? You know that?

Sam: What? You don't? Well, look at the map, Lucy!

b) ● What can you tell the Plymouth kids about Germany? Find information, for example about Germany's biggest towns, lakes, mountains … Write four or more sentences with comparisons.

The Zugspitze is the highest mountain in Germany.

[1] Thames [temz]

7 New neighbours ➜ SB (p. 34)

a) Dan writes an email to a friend about their new neighbours. Read the text.

We have new neighbours. They moved to our street last week. They come from London, so they don't know Plymouth yet. They're OK.

They have a big family, three boys and a girl. The boys' names are Jamie, Jack and Jake. Jamie is 14. He's the oldest, but he isn't the tallest, that's Jack. Jake is the smallest, but he isn't as old as the others. The boys all have brown hair, but Jack's hair is the darkest, and the longest too. It looks cool. He can tell funny jokes and he laughs a lot. I think maybe he's the funniest of the three brothers.

Jack and Jake go to Coombe Dean, but Jamie goes to Plymstock. He's in the same year as me. He has a cool new bike. He goes to school on it. Well, maybe it isn't new, but it's newer than my bike. It's cleaner than my bike too!

We played football together after school. Jamie is good and it was fun. Nick played with us too. He said Jamie was better than me! Well, maybe he is better – just a bit, but Jamie said, "I'm not better than you, Dan. I was just luckier today." He's nice.

Mum says we're going to invite all the family to tea at the weekend. That's great – because the boys' sister is nice too …

b) Choose an answer and circle a letter.
The letters after the correct answers tell you the name of the new family.

1 Jack and Jake are not as old as Jamie **W**. / Jack and Jake are older than Jamie **S**. W
2 Jack is smaller than his brothers **A**. / Jack is taller than his brothers **I**. ___
3 Jake isn't as big as Jamie and Jack **L**. / Jake is bigger than Jamie or Jack **K**. ___
4 Jack is the youngest **L**. / Jake is younger than the others **K**. ___
5 Jamie has darker hair than the others **T**. / Jack's hair is the darkest **I**. ___
6 Jack has longer hair than his brothers **N**. / Jake's hair is the longest **M**. ___
7 Jake is the funniest of the three brothers **E**. / Jack is funnier than his brothers **S**. ___
8 Dan's bike isn't as clean as Jamie's **O**. / Dan's bike is cleaner than Jamie's **F**. ___
9 Dan is better at football than Jamie **Y**. / Dan isn't as good at football as Jamie **N**. ___

c) Who's who? Write the boys' names under the pictures.

___

___

___

8 READING COURSE Reading aloud – An exciting story ➜ SB (p. 35) • SF8 (p. 85)

a) Tick (✓) the correct boxes. When you read aloud, it is important to … :

- understand everything. ◯
- read the text quietly first. ◯
- always read fast. ◯
- know how to pronounce[1] all the words. ◯
- show the writer's feelings (scared, excited, …) in your voice. ◯
- look for punctuation marks (! ? , . :). ◯
- pause in the right places (after , . :). ◯
- look at your friends. ◯

b) 06 Class 8 EB had to write an exciting story for English homework. Justin's camping trip gave Lucas an idea. Here is part of Lucas's story. Read it quietly. Then listen.

Last year, I visited my uncle in Canada. Uncle Tom and my cousin Wayne love camping, and one weekend they took me with them. My first camping trip! Wow! On the way, Uncle Tom told us a scary story about bears, but he said, "Don't worry[2]! There aren't any bears where we're going." I hoped he was right.

Our campsite was great: caravans and tents next to a lake in a forest. In the evening, we sat round a camp fire with other campers. We sang songs and told jokes. It was fun, and I didn't think about bears.

It was windy in the night and I woke up. I could hear strange sounds outside the tent. Maybe it was only the wind in the trees, or maybe it was just another camper – or a wild animal? I tried not to think about Uncle Tom's scary bear story. I closed[3] my eyes and put my hands over my ears.

The next morning I got up early. Uncle Tom was still asleep, but Wayne wasn't in the tent. I got up, took my rucksack with my wash things, and followed the sign to the toilets.

"Yes. That's where Wayne must be," I thought. It was very quiet in the forest, and the tall dark trees looked scary in the early morning light. Suddenly I heard something behind me. I turned round, but there was nothing. Was this the right way? And where was Wayne?

Then I saw something blue under a tree, just a few metres away. What could it be? I walked over to the tree. Then I saw what it was – a blue rucksack! It was Wayne's rucksack. But where was Wayne? Suddenly I had a very bad feeling. Was Uncle Tom wrong about the bears?

…

c) In lines 8–12, mark in blue the places where you can pause. Then listen again and read the lines aloud.

d) How does Lucas feel at different parts of the story? (Circle) the correct answer: **A**, **B** or **C**.

I think the writer feels *happy*:

- **A** I hoped he was right. (l. 7)
- **B** It was fun, and I didn't think about bears. (ll. 11–12)
- **C** Was this the right way? (l. 27)

I think the writer feels *nervous*:

- **A** Our campsite was great: … (l. 8)
- **B** I could hear strange sounds outside the tent. (ll. 13–14)
- **C** "Yes. That's where Wayne must be," I thought. (l. 23)

I think the writer feels *scared*:

- **A** It was windy in the night and I woke up. (l. 13)
- **B** The next morning I got up early. (l. 19)
- **C** Suddenly I heard something behind me. (ll. 25–26)

I think the writer feels *surprised*:

- **A** I turned round, but there was nothing. (ll. 26–27)
- **B** I walked over to the tree. (ll. 30–31)
- **C** Then I saw what it was – a blue rucksack! (l. 31)

e) Read your answers from d) aloud. Practise the sentences with a happy, nervous, scared or surprised voice.

f) 06 Listen to the story again. Practise reading it aloud, slowly, clearly and with feeling.

[1] pronounce [prəˈnaʊns] *aussprechen* [2] worry [ˈwʌri] *sich Sorgen machen* [3] close [kləʊz] *schließen, zumachen*

9 WORDS Stage and film ➜ SB (p. 38)

a) ○ Write the missing words in the puzzle and find the word in the blue boxes.

1 There's a good film at the … this week.
2 Do you play an …? – Yes, I do. I play the guitar.
3 At the auditions, Lucy felt a bit nervous on …
4 Lucy is learning to play the …
5 There's a good … on Saturday. My favourite band!
6 We went to the … to see *Cats*.
7 The teachers chose eight … dancers for *We will rock you*.

➜ The word in the blue boxes is: _ _ _ _ _ _ _ .

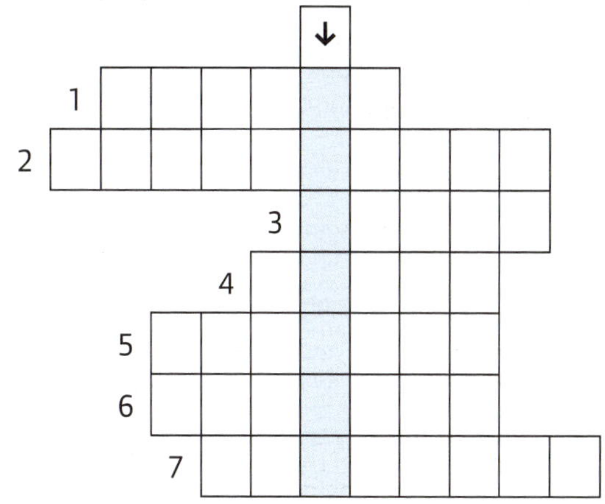

b) ● How many musicals can you think of? Write them down. Which is your favourite and why? Write a short paragraph in your exercise book.

I can think of … musicals. They are: … I like … best because the story/songs/dancing …

10 Which is more exciting? (Comparison of adjectives) ➜ SB (p. 38) • GF6 (p. 91)

What do you think? Compare the things in the pictures with more … than … .

1 

exciting:
I think football/basketball is more exciting than basketball/football.

2 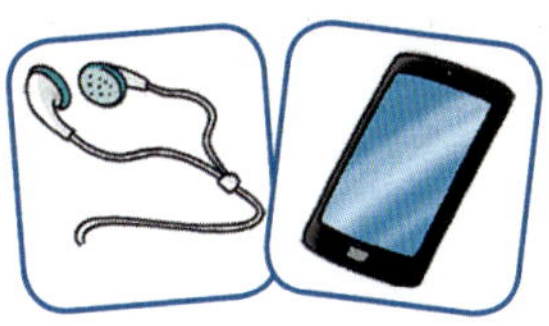

expensive: ____________________

3 

dangerous: ____________________

4 

boring: ____________________

5 

interesting: ____________________

6 

important: ____________________

[1] drama ['drɑːmə] *Schauspiel, darstellende Kunst*

11 The Plymstock auditions (Comparison of adjectives) ➜ SB (p. 38) • GF 6 (p. 91)

Finish the text with the right form of the adjectives. Use a comparison with -er, -est, more or most.

Cats and *Oliver* are good musicals, but Lucy thinks *We will rock you* is the *most exciting* (exciting) musical. It's the ______________ (long) too. Before the audition, Lucy was a bit nervous, but she was much ______________ (nervous) on stage. The second girl's voice was the ______________ (beautiful) of all the singers, but Lucy's voice was ______________ (interesting), ______________ (loud) and ______________ (clear). The teachers thought Leo was the ______________ (talented) dancer, and the ______________ (funny) too. Everybody clapped and cheered.

12 Lucy's email ➜ SB (p. 38) • SF 13 (p. 86)

● After the auditions, Lucy writes an email to her grandparents. Use the notes and finish what she writes. You can add your own ideas too. Lucy writes about:

- *the School Show Club*
- the musical
- the auditions: when and where
- who was there
- the second girl singer
- how she (Lucy) felt on stage
- which song she (Lucy) sang
- Leo and the other dancers
- how she (Lucy) feels now

TIP: Read about the auditions on pp. 36–37 in your student's book again.

Hi, Grandma and Grandpa!

Today was really exciting. I must tell you about it. I'm in the School Show Club now. This year we are going to ...

____

____

____

____

____

Maybe Holly and I can visit you again at the weekend. Then I can tell you more.

Love, Lucy

13 Cinema, theatre or concerts? ➜ SB (p. 38) • SF 15 (p. 87)

● Which do you/your family/your friends like best: the cinema, the theatre or live concerts? Say why. Get ready to talk in class for one minute. Write notes.
Ideas: films, plays, shows, musicals; exciting, interesting, boring, expensive, cheap

I like the cinema better than ... I think ... is the most expensive/the cheapest.
My mum and dad like to go to ...

14 Who was the best? ➔ SB (p. 39) • SF 14 (pp. 86–87)

a) ○ 07 Listen. Where are the speakers? Tick (✓) the correct box.

- ☐ At a party
- ☐ At a music centre in town
- ☐ At the School Music Club

b) Read the sentences. Then listen again and (circle) the right answer.

1	Amira plays the … in her brother's band.	A guitar	B drums	C piano
2	Ranjiv is in … at Coombe Dean.	A Year 8	B Year 9	C Year 10
3	Ranjiv's band was …	A band one.	B band two.	C band three.
4	The singer's name in Ranjiv's band is …	A Ben.	B Bill.	C Will.
5	Nina thinks Band … has the best song and best singer.	A three	B one	C two
6	The second band was … band.	A Harry's	B Ranjiv's	C Steve's
7	The girl singer was in … band.	A Steve's	B Harry's	C Ranjiv's
8	Bands … write their own songs.	A one and two	B two and three	C one and three

15 Whose things are they? (Possessive pronouns) ➔ SB (p. 39)

a) ○ After the geography group work, there were some things on the students' desks. (Circle) the correct word.

Justin: Lucy, I think this ruler is your / (yours).

Lucy: No, it isn't mine / my. But ask Emma. Maybe it's theirs / hers.

Emma: Oh, the yellow ruler is Tom's, I think. Yes, I'm sure it's his / hers.

b) Now finish the sentences with *mine, yours, his, …*

Lucy: Is this your blue pencil, Sam?

Sam: No, it isn't *mine*. Ask Justin. Maybe it's ______________.

Lucy: Justin, is this blue pencil ______________?

Justin: No, it isn't ______________. But Katie had a pencil like that. I think it's ______________.

Lucy: And what about these worksheets? There are no names on them.

Justin: Ask the kids in the group behind us. They must be ______________.

Lucy: Good idea. Hey, Anna and Max. These worksheets are ______________, right?

Anna: Oh, yes. Thanks. They're ______________. We need them for homework.

c) ● Write a dialogue about school things like in b) with a partner.

16 Shrek the Musical ➜ SB (p. 39) • SF 12 (p. 86)

Du bist mit deiner Familie in Plymouth. Deine kleine Schwester und du seht dieses Poster. Ihr würdet gern das Musical besuchen. Mach Notizen auf Deutsch für eure Eltern. Sie wollen bestimmt wissen:

- um was es im Musical geht
- wann die Vorstellungen sind
- was es kostet.
- wo es gespielt wird und wie man hinkommt
- wie lange die Vorstellung dauert

Shrek the Musical (London)

17 STUDY SKILLS A vocabulary picture poster ➜ SB (p. 40) • SF 3 (p. 84)

a) Choose an umbrella word and write your word on the umbrella.

1 sports 2 school clubs 3 theatre 4 musical instruments

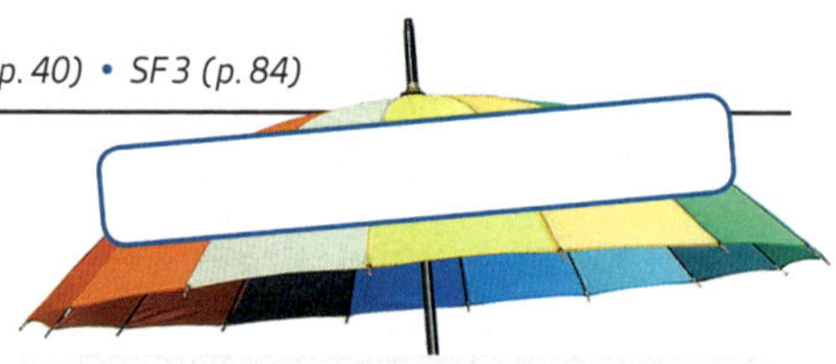

b) Write four or five words under your umbrella word. You can use the WORDBANK in your student's book (pp. 140–141).

c) Draw or find a picture for each word.

d) Think of an idea for a 'picture frame' for your words. Plan, then make your poster.

How to make a good poster
- Make your poster interesting and easy to read: write big, clear words. Check the spelling.
- Use colours for your words.
- Make clear drawings or find good pictures.
- Make sure they go with your words.
- Write words next to or under the correct drawing or picture.

18 TEXT Disco night ➜ SB (pp. 42–43)

a) ○ Read the text on pp. 42–43 of your student's book again. Put the sentences in the right order. Write 1–10 in the boxes.

1 Lucy thinks the Year 7 kids at the disco look funny. ☐
2 The Plymouth kids talk about the school disco night. 1
3 Justin takes a photo of Lucy and Leo on the dance floor. ☐
4 Leo asks Lucy to dance. ☐
5 Sam tells the others why he can't go to the disco. ☐
6 Sam's dad talks to him about school rules. ☐
7 Sam is sad when he sees Justin's photo. ☐
8 Sam and Justin don't want to dance. ☐
9 Lucy is surprised when she sees Sam. ☐
10 Soon Leo is the only dancer on the dance floor. ☐

b) The story has four parts. Which part of the story does the picture show? How do you know? Write a few sentences.

The picture shows a scene from part ...

c) ● Imagine you are Sam. Tell your story about the day of the disco. Write a text (10–12 sentences).

Mrs Taylor sent my parents a note about my phone, so they were angry ...

1 WORDS Free time

Finish the sentences with words from this unit.

1 Maya is going sailing today. The sun is shining, so she needs her **s** u n g l a s s e s.

2 Lucy and her mum are going to a fashion **s** _ _ _ _ in the **t** _ _ _ _ _ _ _ _ on Thursday.

3 Sam's parents have tickets for the **t** _ _ _ _ _ _ today. They're going to see a **p** _ _ _ _.

4 Holly's favourite rock band are giving a **c** _ _ _ _ _ _ at the Plymouth Pavilions on Friday.

5 Justin can't listen to music on the bus because he can't find his **e** _ _ _ _ _ _ _ _.

6 Leo wasn't **n** _ _ _ _ _ _ at the school **a** _ _ _ _ _ _ _ _. He likes to dance on **s** _ _ _ _.

2 Lunchtime (*going to*-future: mixed forms)

Use the correct form of *be going to*.

Justin: So you ____________ (sing) in the show, Lucy, and Leo ____________ (dance).
That's really cool. Which parts ____________ you ____________ (play)?

Lucy: We don't know yet, but we ____________ (play) big parts.

Leo: Wrong! Lucy ____________ (be) a star! ____________ you ____________ (come) and film us, Justin?

3 An email (Comparison of adjectives)

This is part of an email from Sam to a friend in London. Write the underlined sentence parts with a different comparison, but with the same meaning.

<u>Plymouth isn't as big as London</u>, but we like it here now. There are lots of cool places to visit. Mum says <u>Plymouth is quieter than London</u> too. She likes that. We all feel at home. Lily and I have some nice friends. <u>Plymouth isn't as expensive as London</u>, and there are some great shopping malls here. And we love the sea and the Sound. <u>The sea is more exciting than the Thames</u>, and <u>London isn't as sunny and windy as Plymouth</u>. It's good for sailing here.
There's a very nice old part of town. Plymouth's history is very interesting too.
You must come and visit me soon! Do you like the photo?

1 London is *bigger than Plymouth.*

2 London isn't ____________

3 London is ____________

4 The Thames isn't ____________

5 Plymouth is ____________

4 Where are they?

08 Listen to two short dialogues. Where are the speakers? Tick (✓) a box.

1 **A** ☐ In a café **B** ☐ In the school canteen **C** ☐ At home

2 **A** ☐ In a science lesson **B** ☐ In a maths lesson **C** ☐ In a geography lesson

5 After school

a) 09 Listen to the friends. What are they talking about? Tick (✓) a box.

A ☐ Music **B** ☐ Free-time activities **C** ☐ Friends' birthdays

b) 09 Read the sentences and listen to the friends again. Are the sentences right **(R)** or wrong **(W)**?

1 Charlotte's birthday is on the 30th. ☐

2 Her party is from 4:30 to 9:30. ☐

3 She's good at football. ☐

4 She doesn't like fashion shows. ☐

5 The pop group *Flash* is giving a concert on 13th November. ☐

6 The telephone number for concert tickets is 0841 1461446. ☐

7 The cheapest tickets for concerts are £18.50. ☐

8 Nick doesn't go camping. ☐

9 Plymouth Argyle[3] is a basketball team. ☐

10 A taekwondo DVD for Nick isn't a good idea. ☐

Check: Listening

a) Vergleiche deine Antworten mit den Lösungen auf Seite 96 im Workbook.
b) Schätze deine Antworten mit einem grünen oder roten Gesicht ein.

	🙂	☹	
4 Where are they? Hast du verstanden, wo sich die Freundinnen befinden?	○	○	➜ 4
5 After School			
1 Hast du in 5 a) das Hauptgesprächsthema richtig verstanden?	○	○	➜ 5, 6 a
2 Hast du in 5 b) die Zahlen und Daten (z. B. *thirteen, thirtieth*) problemlos verstanden?	○	○	➜ 1
3 Hast du die Uhrzeiten und die Telefonnummer richtig verstanden?	○	○	➜ 2, 3
4 Hast du die Detailfragen richtig beantworten können?	○	○	➜ 6 b

c) Wenn du dich rot eingeschätzt hast, schau dir die rechte Spalte an.
Die Nummern führen dich zu den passenden Übungen im Skills Training (S. 26–27).
Dort kannst du gezielt Hörverstehen trainieren.

[1]background ['bækgraʊnd] *Hintergrund* [2]noise [nɔɪz] *Geräusch, Lärm* [3]Argyle [aː'gaɪl]

1 Numbers ➜ *SF 14 (pp. 86–87)*

a) 10 Listen and (circle) what you hear: one of each pair.

1 50 / 15	3 76 / 67	5 13 / 30	7 15th / 50th
2 30th / 13th	4 45 / 54	6 14 / 40	8 40th / 14th

b) 11 Listen and write what you hear as a number.

1 *40*

2 ______

3 ______

4 ______

5 ______

6 ______

7 ______

8 ______

TIP:

1 Remember:
We say numbers differently!
For example, '43':
German: dreiund**vierzig**
English: **forty**-three

2 Listen for these endings:
fift**een** (15), fift**y** (50),
fift**eenth** (15th), fift**ieth** (50th)

2 Times ➜ *SF 14 (pp. 86–87)*

a) 12 Listen and match. Which times are the same? Draw lines.

A — 6:15

B

C

D

E

F

5:50

6:15

6:30

6:25

6:45

7:30

b) 13 Listen to the students and number the times in the order you hear them. Write 1–8 in the boxes.

☐ ☐ *1* ☐ ☐ ☐ ☐ ☐

3 Telephone numbers ➜ *SF 14 (pp. 86–87)*

14 Listen to the students.
What are their mobile phone numbers?
Write the phone numbers.

Emily: ______ Dan: ______

Amira: ______ Nina: ______

Nick: ______ Charlotte: ______

4 School clubs ➔ SF 14 (pp. 86–87)

15 **Listen to the students. Which clubs do they talk about? Circle A, B or C.**

	A	B	C
1	Science Club	Gardening Club	Computer Club
2	Basketball Club	Reading Club	Football Club
3	Dance Group	Drama Club	School Band

TIP: When you listen, try to concentrate on the **general**[1] meaning. Don't listen for all the details[2].

5 Voicemail messages ➔ SF 14 (pp. 86–87)

16 **Nina has four messages on her voicemail. What are they about? Listen and match.**

Message 1
Message 2
Message 3
Message 4

A the weekend
B homework
C a sports match
D giving a talk

TIP: Before you listen, think about words you need to talk about A–D. Then listen for the words.

Example: school
subjects, books, exercise, break, teachers' names …

6 A radio interview ➔ SF 14 (pp. 86–87)

17 **First read the statements, then listen to part of a radio programme. You can take notes if you want. Are the sentences right or wrong? Tick (✓) a box.**

TIP:
Before you listen:
1 Look at the title and the pictures.
2 Look for **keywords** in the statements. You can mark them.

TIP: Before you listen a **second** time, get ready to take notes in a **table** or **list**.

You don't have to understand every word. Listen for the **keywords**.

	Right	Wrong	
1 Liz is the youngest.	◯	◯	____
2 Anna is the singer.	◯	◯	____
3 Rob plays lead guitar.	◯	◯	____
4 The group made their first demo in 2013.	◯	◯	____
5 Tom plays lead guitar.	◯	◯	____
6 Tom and Liz write the songs.	◯	◯	____
7 Their first single was in the UK charts at number 40.	◯	◯	____
8 The new single is called *Only Maybe*.	◯	◯	____
9 They are doing a concert tour of Great Britain.	◯	◯	____
10 The tour starts in Plymouth on the 30th.	◯	◯	____
11 Liz and Tom like biking.	◯	◯	____
12 Rob likes riding and tennis.	◯	◯	____

[1]general ['dʒenrəl] *allgemein, generell* [2]detail ['diːteɪl] *Einzelheit*

Out and about

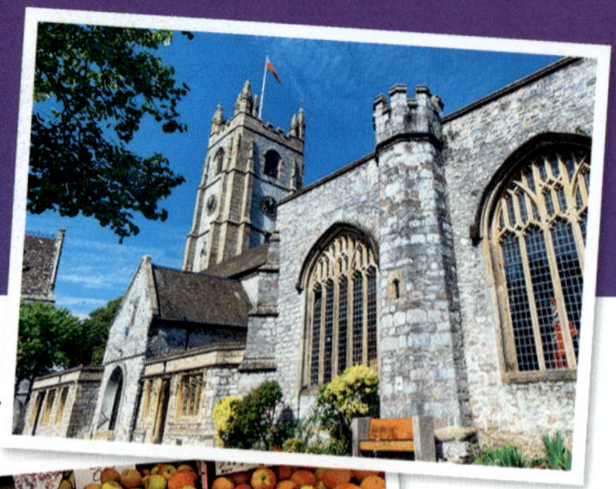

1 WORDS Places in town ➜ SB (pp. 46–47)

a) ○ Which is which? Match and write a letter (A–F) in the boxes (1–6).

1 This is a place where two or more roads meet.
2 This is usually a beautiful, old building where people often go on Sundays.
3 Here you can buy lots of different things from stalls[1], often outside.
4 You can send letters and postcards from here.
5 This is the place where buses arrive and leave.
6 You need time and money here. There's everything in one big area.

A post office
B shopping centre
C church
D bus station
E market
F roundabout

1 F 2 ☐ 3 ☐ 4 ☐ 5 ☐ 6 ☐

b) What other words do you know for places in town? Write at least six more words.

c) ● Take words from b) and write sentences like in a) in your exercise book.
Read the definitions to your partner. He/She has to find the word.

2 Excuse me, can you tell me the way to …? ➜ SB (pp. 46–47) • SF 14 (pp. 86–87)

18 A tourist in Plymouth is in Friars Lane and wants to go to the Elizabethan House in New Street.
Look at the map and listen. Who tells the tourist the right way? The man or the woman? Tick (✓) a box.

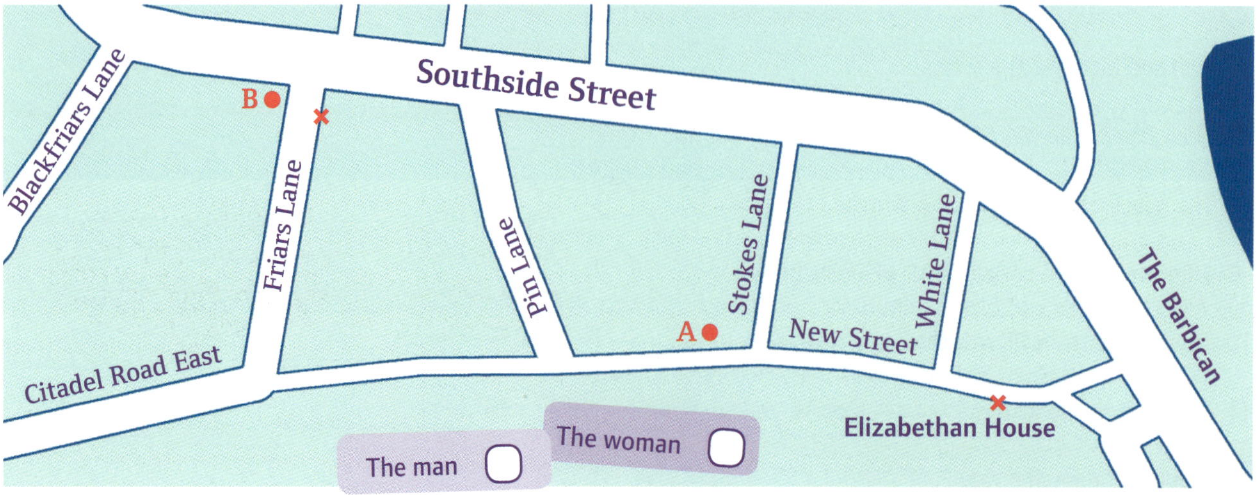

The man ☐ The woman ☐

[1]stall [stɔːl] (Markt-)Stand

3 Telling someone the way ➜ SB (pp. 46-47)

a) ● Look at the map in exercise 2. Dan is in Citadel Road East, almost at the corner of Stokes Lane (point A). Someone asks him the way to the Ice Cream Studio in Southside Street (point B).
Imagine you are Dan. Explain how to get there.

It's in .../Go along.../Go straight on till you come to .../Turn right/left. Go past .../ When you get to .../It isn't far ...

b) 19 Listen and check Dan's answer. There is more than one correct answer.

4 An email to Plymouth ➜ SB (pp. 46–47) • SF 13 (p. 86)

Write an email to a friend from Plymouth and tell him/her about your town.
Use words from exercise 1. Write about 100 words in your exercise book/on the computer.
Plan your email first. Write your notes here.

Hi, Lucy/Sam/...!

I'd like to tell you about my town/village.

I live in ..., near ...

There are lots of ...

In the town centre there's ...

At the weekend you can ...

I like my town because ...

That's all for today. Write soon.

Bye, ...

5 Out and about in my town ➜ SB (pp. 46–47)

Prepare a two-minute speech to tell a new friend about your favourite place in your town or village.
Maybe postcards or photos can help you.
The ideas in your email in exercise 4 can help you too.

- Say what your place has or doesn't have (interesting buildings and places for kids).
- Say what tourists and visitors can do there (see sights, old part of town, buy something, take photos, do a bus tour, go for long walks).

There's a sports centre and two cinemas, but there isn't a theatre.

Tourists like our old town. They can do a bus tour and climb up to the castle.

There's just a church and a few shops in our village, but in the next town there's ...

Make notes in your exercise book or on a crib sheet. You can use them in your short speech.

6 What do they say? (Reporting) ➜ SB (pp. 50–51) • GF 7 (pp. 91–92)

a) Who says what? Match the pictures with the sentences.

2 I go to boarding school now.

5 I'm a cool dancer!

1 I love swimming and sailing.

3 I play basketball with Justin after school.

4 I'm going to sing at the school musical and I can't wait!

b) Report what the kids say.

1 *Maya says she loves swimming and sailing.*

2 ______

3 ______

4 ______

5 ______

7 Text messages from Dan (Reporting) ➜ SB (pp. 50–51) • GF 7 (pp. 91–92)

Imagine you are Dan. Write text messages about what the people say.

1 *Hi Mum. Grandma says she can't come for lunch on Sunday.*

2 ______

3 ______

4 ______

8 EXTRA A lot of things (Paraphrasing) ➜ SB (p. 51) • GF8 (p. 92)

○ Read the sentences 1–7. Then choose and write the correct answer.

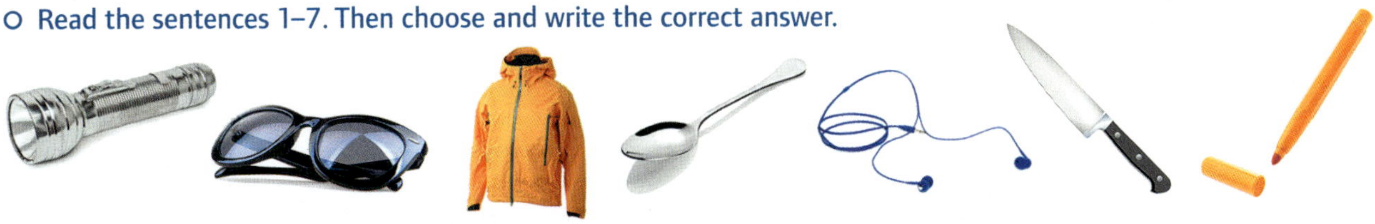

1 It's something that you use when you listen to music on your phone. *earphones*

2 It's something that you wear when it's cold. ____________

3 It's something that you use when you eat soup. ____________

4 It's something that you use when it's dark. ____________

5 It's something that you wear when it's very sunny. ____________

6 It's something that you write with in school. ____________

7 It's something that you use when you prepare your food. ____________

9 EXTRA Who's who? (Paraphrasing) ➜ SB (p. 51) • GF8 (p. 92)

a) Describe and explain who and what you see in the pictures. Use a person/animal/bird and that.

Number 1 *is a person that acts in a theatre or in a film.*

Number 2 ____________

Number 3 ____________

Number 4 ____________

Number 5 ____________

b) ● Explain what or who they are to an English friend who is staying with you. Use relative clauses.

1 Tourist/in: ____________

2 Fähre: ____________

____

3 Taucher/in: ____________

4 Zoowärter/in: ____________

5 Stadtplan: ____________

____

10 See Munich[1]! ➜ SB (p. 51) • SF 12 (p. 86)

● You are in Munich with your family and an English friend. This friend doesn't speak German. Tell him/her a few things about sightseeing tours and three sights. Don't translate. Prepare what you want to say and write it down. You can explain the underlined words with *that*.

Münchener Stadtrundfahrten

Lernen Sie die vielen Sehenswürdigkeiten Münchens kennen! Genießen Sie eine geführte Tour in einem bequemen, vollklimatisierten Reisebus oder erkunden Sie die Isarmetropole im Doppeldeckerbus. Machen Sie mit uns anschließend einen Spaziergang durch die Altstadt. Erfahrene, mehrsprachige Stadtführer/-innen begleiten Sie.
Entdecken Sie u. a. folgende Highlights:

- Schloss Nymphenburg und Schlosspark
- Residenz
- Olympia Park mit Olympiaturm
- den Englischen Garten
- Allianz-Arena
- berühmte Kirchen
- Marienplatz mit Rathaus und Glockenspiel

You can go on different tours. There are lots of 'Sehenswürdigkeiten' – they are things and places that …

11 WORDS A plate of sandwiches ➜ SB (p. 52)

Dan's mum was at the shops. Now she's having a cold lunch. What's on the kitchen table? Use *a bag of …, a basket of …/…* Sometimes, more than one answer can be correct.

On the kitchen table there's …

1 *a of* ______
2 ______
3 ______
4 ______
5 ______
6 ______
7 ______
8 ______
9 ______
10 ______

[1]Munich ['mju:nɪk]

12 Shopping ➜ SB (p. 52)

a) 20 Dan is looking for a present for his sister's birthday. Listen first.

b) 21 Now you are Dan. Listen to the shop assistant and answer the questions. You can record what you say.

c) ● Find a partner and write a dialogue like in b). Write it in your exercise book.

13 READING COURSE Scanning a text ➜ SB (p. 53) • SF 6, 9 (p. 85)

Read the questions, then scan the text for the **keywords**. Answer the questions when you find the information.

1 Are there lots of different **animals**?
2 Can you go there when the **weather** is bad?
3 Are there any exciting **rides**?
4 Can you take your **dog** with you?
5 What about **food** and drinks?
6 Is there a **shop** in the park?

DEVON THEME PARK

NON-STOP FUN FOR ALL THE FAMILY

There's lots of family fun at Devon all-weather adventure park! It has a fantastic indoor play area for kids, so there's lots to do when it's raining.

Visitors love the outdoor centre too, with the Zoo and fun zones. You can choose from 14 great rides and attractions. The rides include the exciting Swing Boat and three fantastic water coasters. There's a play zone for small children and train rides for juniors. There's a big play area for the under 3s too – something for kids of all ages.

Visit over 250 animals, birds and reptiles in the Zoo and Fun Farm. Watch baby rabbits, ponies, snappy baby crocs, meerkats, even pythons – and many more. Don't miss the amazing falcons at the superb Bird Centre. The falcon show with almost 50 birds is a 'must see' for all the family.

Hungry? In the cafés and restaurants you can enjoy delicious food, snacks, salads, sandwiches or a hot lunch. Relax in the Coffee Pot with yummy homemade cakes, a cream tea with homemade jams, or ice cream!

Visit the park shop for souvenirs, postcards, animal posters, games, books and soft toys. Take home a box of special Devon biscuits. There's something for everyone.

Please note that dogs are not allowed in the park.

Call 01803–782958 for more information.

Buy tickets online and save ££££s!

Open every day from March to November from 9:30 am

14 Which is which? (Adjectives and adverbs) ➜ *SB (p. 55) • GF 9 (pp. 92–93)*

○ **Put the words in the snake into two lists.**

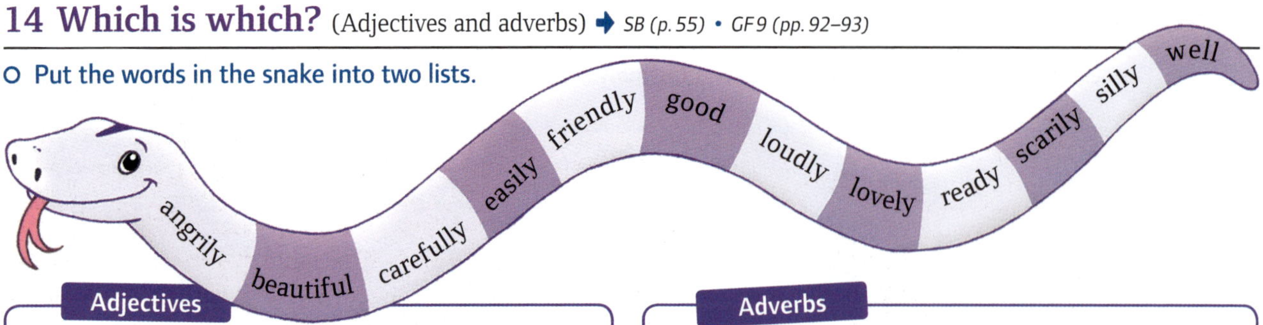

Adjectives	Adverbs

15 Who works well? (Adjectives and adverbs) ➜ *SB (p. 55) • GF 9 (pp. 92–93)*

Do you need an adjective or an adverb? Underline the right word.

The Plymouth kids like school and they're (1 **good/well**) students. Lucy is a (2 **careful/carefully**) student and she works (3 **quietly/quiet**). She's a (4 **well/good**) singer too. At the auditions for the school show she started her song (5 **nervous/nervously**), but she soon sang (6 **loud/loudly**) and (7 **clear/clearly**). The teachers really liked her and she was (8 **happy/happily**). Sam likes geography, but he doesn't always listen (9 **careful/carefully**) in class. Mrs Taylor got (10 **angry/angrily**) because he wore earphones in her lesson. Maya is great at sport and maths. She can always do her homework (11 **easily/easy**). Justin loves his video camera. He talks about his films (12 **excited/excitedly**) when he skypes with his dad in Boston. Leo loves music and he can dance very (13 **good/well**). At the disco everybody cheered (14 **mad/madly**) when they watched him on the dance floor.

16 Sam speaks loudly (Adverbs of manner) ➜ *SB (p. 55) • GF 9 (pp. 92–93)*

Rewrite the sentences with an adjective. Don't change the meaning.

1 Sam speaks loudly. *He speaks in a loud voice.*

2 Maya swims well. ____________________

3 Master Wong fights cleverly. ____________________

4 Maya learns fast. ____________________

5 Lucy sings beautifully. ____________________

6 Maya speaks quietly. ____________________

7 Sam plays basketball well. ____________________

8 Justin works carefully. ____________________

17 Plymouth harbour ➔ SB (p. 55) • SF 6, 9, 11 (pp. 85–86)

a) Before you read, look at the title and the pictures. What do you think the story is about?

· Pilgrims board the Mayflower ·

· Plymouth UK ·
The Mayflower steps today

The sea has always been important for England, so Plymouth harbour is full of history. Many great sailors sailed from there, but the story that people know best is the story of the Mayflower and the people who sailed in her.

On 6th September 1620, the Mayflower left Plymouth harbour for America. On the ship there were 50 men, 20 women and 32 children, about 30 sailors and two dogs. Many of the people were Pilgrims[1], who had a hard life in England at that time. Their lives were in danger because they did not agree with the Church of England and King James I. They wanted to be free to practise their religion differently. They wanted to start a new life in America.

In the first weeks of the voyage[2] the weather was good, but later it was very dangerous. There were awful storms with very high waves. The ship rocked[3] in the water like a toy boat. All the people were sea-sick. The wind howled loudly. Part of the ship broke. Not only the children were scared. Families and friends sat together nervously, and prayed[4]. But there were other problems too. On the decks below, where the Pilgrims spent most of their time, it was cold, wet and dark. There were no windows, no light. Many people slept in one bed, or on the floor. They couldn't walk around freely on the small ship. They didn't have much food. They ate only rice, dried peas, salted fish and salted beef. There were no toilets. There was no water for washing. There was a bad smell everywhere. Also, the sailors were not friendly to the Pilgrims. And so it went on, for 66 days. One sailor died on the ship, and a young man, William Butten, died only two days before the end of the voyage.

The Mayflower arrived in America on 11th November. The Pilgrims wanted to land in Virginia, but there were storms and the sea maps were bad, so they landed 600 miles north of Virginia, at Cape Cod. For the first weeks many of the Pilgrims stayed on the ship, but some got ill and died in the hard winter. Later, the survivors[5] made their new home near a place that is today Plymouth, Massachusetts. You can visit Plymouth Rock, the place where British people arrived in America almost four hundred years ago.

b) Read the statements. Are they right (R), wrong (W), or is the information not in the text (N)?

1 The Mayflower sailed from Plymouth at the end of September. [W]

2 There were more than a hundred people on board. [ ]

3 The ship was 12 years old. [ ]

4 The Pilgrims were not happy with the king and the church. [ ]

5 In the first few days, there was a dangerous storm at sea. [ ]

6 Life on the ship was very hard. [ ]

7 The Mayflower had three decks. [ ]

8 Three people died on the voyage. [ ]

9 The ship landed on the coast of Virginia. [ ]

10 The Pilgrims called their new home 'Plymouth'. [ ]

> **TIP:**
> 1 Read all the statements first and mark **keywords**.
> 2 Scan the text and look for the keywords.
> 3 Read the sentence parts **around the keywords** to find the correct information.

[1]Pilgrim ['pɪlgrɪm] *Pilger/in* [2]voyage ['vɔɪɪdʒ] *Seereise* [3]rock [rɒk] *schaukeln* [4]pray [preɪ] *beten* [5]survivors [sə'vaɪvəz] *Überlebende*

18 Let's go to … ➜ SB (p. 55) • SF 15 (p. 87)

a) 22 You meet Nina and Dan in Plymouth. You want to do something together. Listen to Nina and Dan and answer their questions about different places and activities. Say two or more sentences for each question.

Say where you would/wouldn't like to go and why.
Say what you would/wouldn't like to do and why.

…

Nina: What about Smeaton's Tower?

You: *Oh, great! That's a good idea. We can climb up the tower and take some cool photos.*

Or: *No, I wouldn't like to go up the tower. It's boring. And there are usually lots of tourists there.*

☺
Yes, that's a good idea.
Yes, that's always fun.
I think it's better than …
Yes, I'd like to do that.
Then we could …
There's a very nice …
Let's do that!

☹
No, I wouldn't like to …
I don't agree. I don't think …
I have to go home soon.
I like … better.
No, I don't like that idea.
It's too far/expensive/boring.
I'm not very good at …

b) ● Now do this exercise again with a partner. This time, talk about places and activities in your town or village. You can take notes in your exercise book.

19 STUDY SKILLS Study posters ➜ SB (p. 56) • SF 4 (p. 84)

a) Make a study poster about the comparison of adjectives.
→ *Looking at language/Language help* in your student's book (pp. 34, 38)
→ *GF 6 Comparison of adjectives* in your student's book (pp. 163–164)

Read Morph's tips before you start:

→ Use a big piece of paper!
→ Write a title at the top of the page (CAPITAL LETTERS).
→ Make your sentences short.
→ Use different colours to mark important words or phrases.
→ Underline important words or phrases.
→ Don't forget examples!
→ Make your poster look interesting, maybe funny.
→ Use drawings and/or pictures.

Now go to the Grammar File 6 (pp. 163–164) and find ideas for your poster text.

b) ● EXTRA Choose another grammar topic and make one more study poster.

20 TEXT Master Wu and the magic book ➜ SB (pp. 58–59) • SF 13 (p. 86)

a) Read pp. 58-59 in your student's book again. Put the pictures in the right order. Write 1–4 in the boxes.

b) What is happening? What are the kids doing? Write two or three sentences for each picture.

In picture 1, *Sam and Leo are standing in front of the open door of the gatehouse. Justin ...* ______

______

In picture 2, ______

______

In picture 3, ______

______

In picture 4, ______

______

c) How do the kids feel in the different parts of the story? Write five or more sentences in your exercise book.

I think Sam/... feels ... when ...

Describing people and feelings:
awful · excited · happy · lucky · nervous · responsible · scared · shocked · worried

d) ● Do you like the story? Why or why not? Prepare to tell the class.

I (don't) like the story because ... The story ...

Describing the story:
exciting · clever · interesting · silly · scary · happy ending

e) ● Write Lucy's diary about what happened in the park. Write 100 words or more in your exercise book.

Something really exciting happened today. Maya and I went to Radford Park. The boys wanted to film some scenes there. We ...

1 PRONUNCIATION Silent[1] letters

23 In each word there are letters which you do not pronounce[2]. Say each word carefully and underline the letters you don't pronounce. You can record[3] your voice. Then listen and check.

1 straight on 2 theatre 3 chocolates 4 juice 5 souvenirs 6 whisper

2 WORDS Nina in town

a) What does Nina have to buy today? Write it down.

1 
____

2 
____

3 
____

b) Where does she have to go? Write correct words.

1 tpreiadesn enoz _______________

2 tpso ifceof _______________

3 pgnsipho rteecn _______________

3 Master Wu and the magic book (Reporting)

Report what the Plymstock kids say when they are at Radford Park.

1 Justin: "The boat is old and broken." *Justin says the boat is old and broken.*

2 Leo: "I can do that." _______________

3 Sam: "I can't feel my legs." _______________

4 Maya: "I'm going in." _______________

4 In a sports shop

a) 24 Nina is in a sports shop. Listen to the dialogue two or three times.

b) 25 Now you are Nina. Listen again and talk to the shop assistant.

[1]silent ['saɪlənt] *still, ruhig* [2]pronounce [prə'naʊns] *aussprechen* [3]record [rɪ'kɔːd] *aufnehmen*

5 Telling someone the way

a) You are in Plym Road (A). A girl asks you the way to a phone shop. Tell her how to get there.

b) You are in Old Road (B). A tourist wants to buy some postcards. Tell him the way to the souvenir shop.

6 Where you live

a) You are in Plymouth with Nina and Dan. Tell them about your town/village and local area. Tell them how it is different from Plymouth. Say ten or more sentences.

b) 26 Now listen and answer Nina and Dan's questions about where you live.

Check: Speaking

a) Vergleiche deine Antworten mit den Lösungen auf Seite 96 im Workbook.
b) Schätze deine Antworten mit einem grünen oder roten Gesicht ein.

	🙂	☹	
1 PRONUNCIATION Silent letters Konntest du die Wörter richtig und ohne Probleme aussprechen?	○	○	→ 1
4 In a sports shop Konntest du nützliche Phrasen/Wörter für ein Einkaufsgespräch verstehen und richtig anwenden? (z. B. *How much does it cost? Have you got …?*)	○	○	→ 2a, b
5 Telling someone the way Konntest du notwendige Phrasen/Wörter für die Wegbeschreibung richtig und flüssig anwenden? (z. B. *Go along …, turn right/left, opposite, between*)	○	○	→ 3, 4
6 Where you live 1 Sind dir die Wörter zur Beschreibung von Stadt und Land (z. B. *church, shopping centre, station, hills, river*) eingefallen und konntest du sie richtig aussprechen?	○	○	→ 5a
2 Konntest du mehrere Sätze über deinen Wohnort spontan und frei sprechen?	○	○	→ 5b, c

c) Wenn du dich rot eingeschätzt hast, schau dir die rechte Spalte an. Die Nummern führen dich zu den passenden Übungen im Skills Training (S. 40–41). Dort kannst du gezielt Speaking trainieren.

1 PRONUNCIATION Mark the letters ➜ SF 14 (pp. 86–87)

27 Mark the letters that you do not pronounce. Then listen and say the words again.

1 chocolate	4 clothes	7 neighbour	10 guitar
2 building	5 castle	8 interesting	11 fruit
3 different	6 juice	9 biscuits	12 straight on

2 WORDS Shopping ➜ SF 15 (p. 87)

a) Match the shopping phrases.

TIP: Learn the phrases by heart[1]. Make sure that you can say them fluently[2].

1 Haben Sie Schreibhefte?

2 Wieviel kosten die?

3 Welche Farben gibt es?

4 Kann ich so eins in Rot haben?

5 Ist das alles?

6 Ich hätte auch gern eine Packung Filzstifte.

7 Wo ist die Kasse?

8 Und £1.25 zurück.

How much are they?

Is that everything then?

Can I have one of those in red, please?

What colours have you got?

Do you have exercise books, please?

Where's the cash desk, please?

Here's your change, £1.25.

I'd like a packet of felt tips too.

b) Practise a shopping dialogue with a partner.
A is the shop assistant. **B** wants to buy a red T-shirt, size 'M', and a blue bag.
Use similar phrases to the phrases in a). Take turns and act your dialogue in class.

A: *Hello. Can I help you? ...* **B:** *Yes, please. Do you have ...*

3 The way home ➜ SF 15 (p. 87)

a) Finish the sentences.

1 Geh die Straße entlang. → Go __________ the street.
2 Überquer die Straße. → __________ the road.
3 Bieg nach links ab. → __________ left.
4 Geh geradeaus. → Go __________.
5 Geh an der Kirche vorbei. → Go __________ the church.
6 Auf der rechten Seite. → __________ right.

b) Tell a partner the way to your home from your school.
First, make a street plan and notes in your exercise book.
You can use phrases from the box.

take a bus ... · get off at ... · go by bike · a long way · not far · easy to find

Here is an example:

You take the bus from the school to Blumenstraße. Get off the bus there.
Go along Blumenstraße, past the post office and the shops. Turn left into ..., then right into ...
When you see ..., cross the road. Walk along ... for about five minutes. Our house is number ...
It's on the right/left.

[1]by heart [baɪ 'hɑːt] *auswendig* [2]fluently ['fluːəntli] *flüssig*

4 Where are they?

Look at the street map in exercise 5 a) (p. 39) again and answer the questions.
Try to use all the words in the box. There is more than one correct answer.

near · next to · between · opposite · on the corner of

1 Where's the post office? *It's in New Street, near* ______

2 Where's the sandwich shop? ______

3 Where's the card shop? ______

4 Where's the bike shop? ______

5 Where's the café? ______

5 Compare the pictures ➜ *SF 17 (p. 87)*

a) What can you see? Write six or more words for each picture. Think of more words and add them to your lists.

In the country: *hills,* ______

______

In a town: *post office,* ______

______

b) What do you think is better: life in a town or life in the country?
Make notes first. Say six sentences or more.

TIP: Remember to use ***and***, ***but***, ***because***, ***when***, ***so*** to make better sentences.

I think life in ... is better than life in ...

Town: *more exciting,* ______

______

Country: *quieter,* ______

______

On Dartmoor

1, 2

1 WORDS On the moor ➜ SB (pp. 66–67)

a) ○ Find the missing words and write them in the puzzle.

1 A … is a farm animal which eats grass.

2 A … is a farm animal which gives us milk.

3 Dartmoor's … is open, wild and beautiful.

4 A … is an area of land in the country. Animals eat grass here.

5 A … is an area of land between hills or mountains.
A river often runs through here.

6 … often live in mountain areas or on farms.
They give us milk.

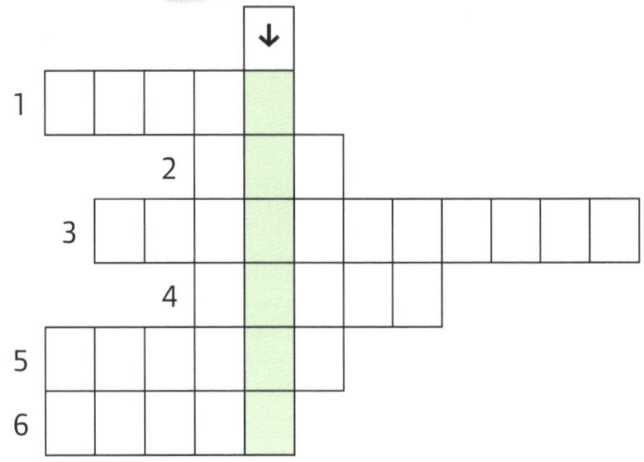

b) ○ Now write the word in the green boxes.

➜ You can see them on Dartmoor: _ _ _ _ _ _ .

2 A picture of Dartmoor ➜ SB (p. 67) • SF 17 (p. 87)

a) Describe Maya's picture of Dartmoor. Say what's in it and where things are.
Write a paragraph.

Use these phrases:
at the top/bottom ·
on the left/right ·
in the middle ·
in the foreground/background

The picture shows the Dartmoor countryside in spring or summer. At the top, there's

b) ● Find a picture from a magazine which shows countryside (mountains, hills, lake, forest, coast, animals, people). Prepare to describe your picture to a partner in a short talk.
Take notes in your exercise book and give your talk. Your partner has to draw what you describe.
Did you describe your picture clearly and well?

3 They've arrived at the farm (Present perfect: regular verbs) ➜ SB (p. 70) • GF 10 (p. 93)

What has happened? Look at the pictures and write a sentence. Use the present perfect.

1 The kids *have arrived at the farm.* ____

2 Lucy *has* ____

3 Sam ____

4 The kids ____

5 The boys ____

6 The girls ____

7 The boys ____

8 Grandpa ____

4 I've done that lots of times! (Present perfect: irregular verbs) ➜ SB (p. 70) • GF 10 (p. 93)

Write sentences about yourself.

I've I haven't	been to eaten fallen seen won written	off my bike the USA a snake a poem in English Indian food a prize	once twice three times a few times lots of times

1 *I've been to the USA once./I haven't been to the USA.*

2 ____

3 ____

4 ____

5 ____

6 ____

5 Sam has fallen in the mud (Present perfect: statements) ➜ SB (p. 70) • GF 10 (p. 93)

Finish sentences 1–5 with the verb in the present perfect.
Then add the correct sentence from the box.

The roast beef looks great. · *Now he has to have a bath.* · Sam doesn't think they're funny. · Oh dear. There aren't any for Grandpa now. · So now they know more about farm animals.

1 Sam *has fallen* in the mud (fall). *Now he needs to have a bath.*

2 Justin ______ some photos of Sam in the mud (take). ______

3 The Plymouth kids ______ all the scones (eat). ______

4 The boys ______ a tour of the farm (have). ______

5 Grandma ______ lunch (make). ______

6 He hasn't done that yet (Present perfect: *already, not … yet*) ➜ SB (p. 71) • GF 9 (pp. 92–93)

Dan's parents aren't at home today. Look at the 'to do' list for Dan and his sister Gemma.
What have they **already** done? What **haven't** they done **yet**? Write it down.

1 *Dan has already fed Charlie.*

2 ______

3 ______

4 ______

5 ______

6 ______

7 What have they just done? (Present perfect: *just*) ➜ SB (p. 71) • GF 10 (p. 93)

What have they **just** done? Finish the sentences.
Use a verb from the box in the present perfect and **just**.

buy · clean · feed · leave home · *make*

1 
2 
3 
4 
5 

1 It smells good in the kitchen. Nina *has just made a chocolate cake.*

2 Nick's bike looks like new. He ______

3 Amira and Emily are going on a bike trip. They ______

4 Charlie isn't hungry. Dan ______

5 Charlotte and her cousin are going to a concert. They ______

8 Back at home (Present perfect: questions with … *yet?*) ➜ SB (p. 73) • GF 10 (p. 93)

Sam and Justin are back in Plymouth after their visit to the Tizzards' farm. Sam's mum asks Sam questions with *Have you … yet?* Read Sam's answers. Then write his mum's questions.

1 *Have you phoned Lucy yet?*	Phoned Lucy? Yes, I have.
2 ______	Washed my dirty clothes? Who, me?
3 ______	Cleaned my muddy boots? Well, er …
4 ______	Yes, I've shown Dad my photos.
5 ______	Yes, I've told Dad about the ride on the tractor. It was cool.
6 ______	Written a thank-you letter to the Tizzards? Why? I've already thanked them.
7 ______	Done my weekend homework? No, I haven't. I've been on the farm all day!

9 Have you ever done that? (Present perfect: questions with … *ever?*) ➜ SB (p. 73) • GF 10 (p. 93)

a) Look at the pictures and write questions.

1 

2 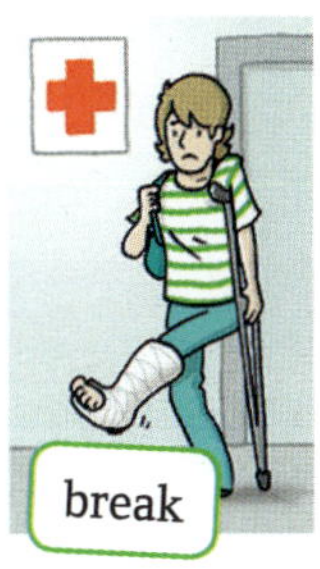

3 

4 

5 

6 

1 *Have you ever tried goat's milk?*

2 ______

3 ______

4 ______

5 ______

6 ______

b) ● Write two funny questions with *Have you ever …?* to ask in class.

1 ______

2 ______

10 READING COURSE Marking up a text ➜ SB (p. 74) • SF 11 (p. 86)

a) Read the text about Dartmoor National Park. Mark keywords and phrases which help you to answer the five questions. Use five different colours.

1 What is Dartmoor NP?
2 What does it look like?
3 Why is Dartmoor sometimes scary?
4 What can you do there?
5 Where can you stay?

Dartmoor is a very large area of wild, open countryside, which has been a national park since 1951. It has almost one thousand square kilometres of moor, hills, trees and rivers. It is famous for its stone circles, stone crosses and its many granite tors.

It's a wild, lonely, mysterious place. In the cold months when it's windy and misty, or when the moors are covered with snow, it's even scary: no houses, no cars, no people. There are lots of old stories about strange happenings, ghosts and phantoms, even killer hounds with eyes like fire. These stories are fascinating for tourists. Have you ever read the story of Sherlock Holmes and *The Hound of the Baskervilles*?

Dartmoor is an amazing place for an active outdoor holiday. There's lots to do there. Watch wildlife, birds and butterflies. Go walking or biking. Other popular activities are swimming, fishing, canoeing and climbing. Dartmoor is perfect for horse riding and pony trekking. You can visit old towns, villages, castles and churches, museums and artists' studios, even England's highest waterfall at Canonteign. The visitor centres can give you lots of information and help you to plan your stay.

If you want to stay overnight, many local farms give visitors a warm welcome and a delicious hot breakfast. Children are often allowed to help with the animals or drive a tractor. In addition, visitors can choose friendly bed and breakfast places, or excellent hotels for their stay. Or why not camp – and read scary stories about ghosts and hounds …?

b) Scan the text to find the words in the box. What helps you to understand their meaning? Write each word in one of the lists. Some words can go in more than one list.

amazing · artist · active · drive · excellent · famous · stone · crosses · granite · mysterious · misty · trekking · covered · happenings · phantoms · popular · killer hounds · fascinating · canoeing

The context helps with these words:	The pictures help with these words:	I know a part of these words:	Similar to a German word:	Similar to words in another language:

c) ● Use your keywords and the parts that you have marked to tell your partner about Dartmoor National Park.

11 Nick's project *(some and any)* ➜ *SB (p. 78) • GF 12 (p. 94)*

Finish the dialogue. Add some or any.

Nick: I have to do a project about Dartmoor for school. Our teacher has given me *some* worksheets, but they're boring. You've been to Dartmoor. Do you have *any* interesting books that can help me?

Amira: I'm sure Dad has __________ maps, but we don't have __________ books. You need __________ brochures[1]. I don't think we have __________, but you can get __________ from the visitor centre.

Nick: OK. But I need __________ photos too. Do you have __________ postcards or photos of tors or stone[2] circles[3]?

Amira: Let me think. Now, where's my old photo box? Erm, … Here it is. Ah, yes. There are __________ photos of Dartmoor.

Nick: Oh, great! Are there __________ that I could use? I'd like __________ pictures of the lonely countryside.

Amira: No, there aren't __________ photos of tors or stone circles, but here's one of Ranjiv trying to ride a cow!

Nick: Oh, yes, that's really cool – but maybe not for my project, Amira …

12 A Dartmoor story: The phantom cottage *(something, anything, …)* ➜ *SB (p. 78) • GF 12 (p. 94)*

Finish the story with something, somebody, anything or anybody.

Years ago, a woman went to live near Islington on Dartmoor, in a house near the forest. She didn't know ______________ in the village. One day on a walk, she saw a lovely little cottage through the trees, but she couldn't see ______________ in it. Later, she asked the landowner[4] about the cottage, but he said there was no cottage on his land, there wasn't ______________, only trees. Ten years later, ______________ built[5] a house on the land. They saw the little cottage, and ______________ at the window, but they couldn't find a door. They asked the village people about it, but they didn't know ______________ about a cottage in the forest. A long time after, a surveyor[6] was in the area and he also saw the cottage far away through the trees. Because the cottage wasn't on his map, he went there again in the evening to find the exact place. But ______________ was very strange. He looked and looked, but he couldn't find the cottage … Why didn't people know ______________ about the cottage? Why didn't ______________ see it a second time?

[1]brochure ['brəʊʃə] *Broschüre* [2]stone [stəʊn] *Stein* [3]circle ['sɜːkl] *Kreis* [4]landowner ['lændəʊnə] *Grundbesitzer* [5]build [bɪld] *bauen* [6]surveyor [sə'veɪə] Landvermesser

13 EXTRA I've been there (Present perfect or simple past) ➜ SB (p. 78) • GF 10–11 (pp. 93–94)

● Finish the dialogue with verb forms in the present perfect or simple past.

Dan: *Have* you *ever been* (ever, be) to Dartmoor, Amira?

Amira: Yes, I have. I ______ (be) there twice. We ______ (be) there last August. We ______ (stay) at a farmhouse. What about you? ______ you ______ (ever, stay) on a farm?

Dan: No, I ______ (never, do) that. I ______ (want) to go to Dartmoor last summer, but my mum and sister like sun and sea more than muddy moors. So we ______ (have) a holiday flat in Italy last year. But Dartmoor is great for riding. ______ you ______ (go) riding when you ______ (be) there?

Amira: No, I didn't. I ______ (never, learn) how to ride.

Dan: So you ______ (never, ride) a wild Dartmoor pony?

Amira: That's right. I haven't.

Dan: Lucky ponies!

14 A postcard from Dartmoor ➜ SB (p. 78) • SF 13 (p. 86)

● Imagine you are having a holiday with your family on a Dartmoor farm. Write a postcard to an English cousin. Tell him/her what you have done/seen so far and what you haven't done/seen yet.
The text in exercise 10 (p. 46) and the ideas in the box can help you.

Write six or more sentences.

> have bacon and eggs · try goat's milk · make scones · take photos · ride on a tractor · see Dartmoor ponies/lambs · feed pigs and cows · have a riding lesson · see birds and butterflies

Dear ______,

We are staying on a Dartmoor farm. I have done lots of cool things so far. Just imagine! Yesterday I fed pigs and cows!

______

______

______

______

______

______

______

Love, ______

To ______

______

______

______

______

15 Zak at work ➜ SB (p. 78) • SF 6, 9 (p. 85)

a) Before you read, look at the title and the photos.

Zak is a pet, but he is also a very special[1] dog. He is one of only thirty dogs in England that can rescue people. Zak is a search[2] dog with the Dartmoor Rescue Group. His workplace is the moor.

Zak loves looking for missing people – and finding them. It's his favourite game, but he doesn't know how important this game is. When people go walking, biking or climbing on the moors, things can go wrong. They can fall and get hurt, or they lose their way and need help. Often their mobile phones don't work on the moors. The weather on Dartmoor can change from sunny to stormy very quickly, and when it gets dark, it is very hard for rescuers to find people. That's why they train dogs.

Zak is a very clever sniffer dog. He runs around in the search area and sniffs the air[3]. He can run for miles across the moor. He looks behind rocks and under bushes. He works in good and bad weather. When he has found somebody, he barks and shows his trainer the way to the missing person.

Zak became a sniffer dog on Dartmoor a few years ago. Before this, he had to do lots of training and tests. He had to learn to walk, sit, lie, wait, come to his trainer when he called him, and all this in stormy weather and in the dark. He has been on more than sixty call-outs with the Plymouth team and has helped to rescue many people. One person was an 18-year-old boy, Nathan. Zak found Nathan near Bench Tor – alone, with a broken leg.

'My brother has gone to find help,' Nathan told the rescue team. 'It's very lonely here. We haven't seen anybody all day. Our mobiles don't work. I was really scared when it got dark. I've never been so cold and wet, and my leg hurts. My brother Matt wanted to find the campsite at Cockingford Farm and get help, that's just two or three miles away. But maybe he's lost in the dark and needs help too.'

The team took Nathan to the ambulance[4], which drove him to hospital. Zak stayed with his trainer and two others. They looked for Matt in the whole area, and Zak found him an hour later. Well done, Zak! Another good day's work.

b) What do you think the underlined words mean in German? Write the answers in your exercise book.

c) What does the text tell us about Zak? Scan the text and make notes in your exercise book.

d) ● Answer the questions in a few sentences.

1 What can happen to visitors on the moors? Name two things.

____

____

____

2 Why do rescue teams need dogs like Zak?

____

____

3 What happened to Nathan and his brother?

____

____

____

[1] special ['speʃl] [2] search ['sɜːtʃ] [3] air [eə] [4] ambulance ['æmbjələns]

16 It happened on Dartmoor ➜ SB (p. 78) • SF 14 (pp. 86–87)

a) 28 Dan, Nina and Nick are talking. Before you listen, look at the title and the pictures. What do you think the friends are talking about? Write it down.

____

b) Read the sentences below. Listen again. Are the statements right (R), wrong (W) or is the information not mentioned[1] (N)?

1 Dan is reading a Sherlock Holmes story. R

2 Nina can remember all the story well. ☐

3 In the story, Sir Charles Baskerville is found dead. ☐

4 Henry Baskerville asks Sherlock Holmes for help. ☐

5 Holmes and his friend Dr Watson go to Dartmoor. ☐

6 Holmes and Watson find the hound. ☐

7 Agatha Christie was from Devon. ☐

8 She wrote her first book in a hotel on Dartmoor. ☐

9 The background of one book is Sittaford on Dartmoor. ☐

10 Agatha Christie wrote lots of stories, but not plays. ☐

11 Agatha Christie died in 1967. ☐

Agatha Christie

An actor as Sherlock Holmes in *The Hound of the Baskervilles*

17 National park rules ➜ SB (p. 79) • SF 12 (p. 86)

● You are on holiday in a national park with a friend from England. Tell him/her in English what you can/can't do and what you have to do there. Don't translate. Use short, easy sentences in your own words. Just say what is important.

There are some important rules in national parks. For example, you can ... but you can't ... You have to ...

1 
Machen Sie bitte kein Feuer. Auch bei Kälte nicht. Jedes Jahr verliert der Park wertvolle Waldflächen durch Brände.

2 
Nehmen Sie Ihren Abfall mit. Nutzen Sie bitte die Abfalleimer, die sich auf den Parkplätzen befinden.

3 
Lassen Sie Ihren Hund im Park nicht frei laufen. Leinen[2] Sie ihn bitte an. Setzen Sie Ihren Hund auf unbekanntem Terrain und auch die Parktiere keiner unnötigen Gefahr aus.

4 
Zelten Sie bitte nur auf den offiziellen Zeltplätzen, die auf Ihrer Nationalpark-Karte gekennzeichnet sind.

5 
Wanderwege zu den schönsten Aussichtspunkten sind ausgeschrieben. Bleiben Sie bitte auf diesen Wegen. Abseits der beschilderten Wege können Gefahren lauern.

[1] mention ['menʃn] *erwähnen* [2] *Hundeleine* leash [liːʃ] or lead [liːd]

18 STUDY SKILLS Describing a picture ➔ SB (p. 79) • SF 17 (p. 87)

● What does the picture show?
Who's in the picture? Where are they?
What are they wearing? Talk about the time of year and the atmosphere[1].
What's happening? Who's doing what?
How do you think the people feel?
Take notes in your exercise book and prepare to tell a partner.

The picture shows a scene ...

19 TEXT The tulip garden ➔ SB (pp. 80–81) • SF 13 (p. 86)

a) Read the text on pp. 80–81 of your student's book again. Choose the correct endings (A–H). Write a letter in the boxes 1–8 below.

1 The girls had hot baths
2 Grandpa told the story of the old woman
3 The old woman was never lonely
4 Pixies danced in the old woman's garden
5 The man grew vegetables in the garden
6 The man put a fence around the garden
7 The man left the cottage
8 Now the cottage is just a ruin

because

A he didn't like flowers and grass.
B she was kind and they liked her.
C they were cold and wet after their adventure.
D he didn't want animals to go in.
E the girls didn't know it.
F nobody moved in after the man.
G children and animals often came to visit her.
H nothing grew there, not even grass.

1 *C* 2 ☐ 3 ☐ 4 ☐ 5 ☐ 6 ☐ 7 ☐ 8 ☐

b) ● Tell the story in about ten sentences. Use simple past forms. Join short sentences with **and**, **but**, **because**, **so**.

A long time ago, an old woman lived ________________

____

____

____

____

____

____

c) ● Do you like this Dartmoor story? Why or why not? Write a few sentences in your exercise book.

I (don't) like this story because ...

[1] atmosphere ['ætməsfɪə]

1 WORDS On the moor

Finish the text with words from this unit.

1 The **c** _ _ _ _ _ _ _ _ _ _ on Dartmoor is beautiful at all times of the year.

2 In spring and summer, there are **f** _ _ _ _ s of green **g** _ _ _ _, where you see lots of **s** _ _ _ _, **c** _ _ s and Dartmoor ponies. There are hills and **v** _ _ _ _ _ s too.

3 The Plymouth kids had a great day on the Tizzards' farm. Sam got **d** _ _ _ _ because he fell in the **m** _ _, so he had to take a **b** _ _ _.

4 There were seven **s** _ _ _ _ **l** _ _ _ _ in Grandpa's **b** _ _ _. They weren't **s** _ _ _ _ _ enough to live alone on the moor. Maya left the barn door open and soon one lamb was **m** _ _ _ _ _ _. The girls went to find it.

5 After their **a** _ _ _ _ _ _ _ _ on the moor in the **h** _ _ _ _ rain, they drank big **m** _ _ s of hot **c** _ _ _ _.

2 Nina has been there (Present perfect)

Finish the dialogue with verb forms in the present perfect or simple past.

Nick: ______________________ (you, ever, be) to Okehampton, Nina?

Nina: Yes, I have. It's on Dartmoor. ______________ (I, stay) there last summer. My mum loves it.

Nick: What about Berry Pomeroy Castle or Dartmouth Castle? ______________________ (you, ever, see) there last year too?

Nina: No, I haven't. I ______________________ (I, never, visit) those castles, but I'd like to.

3 Let's find it!

Read the text and mark important words and phrases. What is the text about?

The text is about ______________________.

Everybody loves a treasure hunt[1], and a hunt across the wild Dartmoor countryside can be fun. People call it 'letterboxing'. You follow clues[2] and look for letterboxes. This popular activity began on Dartmoor in 1854 and has become an exciting outdoor hobby for people of all ages.

A 'letterbox' is a waterproof container, which can be a tin or a metal or plastic box. In the container there's a stamp, with the name of the tor or place, and a visitors' book. When you find a letterbox, you put the stamp into your own note-book and write your name or put your own stamp in the visitors' book. There are hundreds of letterboxes on Dartmoor. People have hidden them in lots of different places: in fields where sheep and cows graze, near tors, in the grass, in farmhouse barns, and in villages too.

Letterboxing began on Dartmoor but now tourists and visitors do it in areas all over the world. Where can you letterbox in your country? Have you ever been letterboxing?

[1]treasure hunt ['treʒə hʌnt] *Schatzsuche* [2]clue [kluː] *Hinweis*

4 Buckfast otters and butterflies

a) First read the sentences 1–8 in b) and mark keywords.
Then scan the text for the keywords and mark the answers.

Opening times
April – October 10:00 am – 5:00 pm daily

What you can see
Find out about three different kinds of otters. Visit the North American otters. You can watch them when they're feeding. Bring your camera because they love it when you take photos! The Asian otters are the smallest, but they are very playful and they make lots of noise. The British otters are shy. They like to live alone. You don't often see them in the wild, so come and visit them here. You can watch them swim in the underwater viewing area. Otters are very fast swimmers. It's fun to watch them swim, play and eat!

Feeding times
The otters feed every day at 11:30 am, 2:00 pm and 4:30 pm. Visitors love to watch them – and they're always hungry. The otter keepers explain the different kinds of otters and answer all your questions. Please don't try to touch the otters or feed them. They bite! You can also spend a morning with a keeper at the 'Otter experience'. Find out much more about these lovely creatures and the work of their keepers.

Butterfly house
Visit the tropical garden with exotic flowers, plants and trees. This rainforest area is the perfect home for many beautiful butterflies.

b) Are the sentences right (R), wrong (W) or is the information not in the text (N)?

1 You can learn about three kinds of otters. ☐
2 North American otters like to live alone. ☐
3 Otters from Asia love to play. ☐
4 British otters like to have people around them. ☐
5 Most otters live three to four years in the wild. ☐
6 There are four feeding times every day. ☐
7 Otters usually live in large groups. ☐
8 There are tropical temperatures, trees and plants in the butterfly house. ☐

c) Mark keywords in the questions. Then answer the questions in a sentence each. Write in your exercise book.

1 How are British otters different from North American and Asian otters?
2 When is the last feeding time?
3 What is the 'Otter experience'?
4 When can you see the otters in summer?

Check: Reading

a) Vergleiche deine Antworten mit den Lösungen auf Seite 96 im Workbook.
b) Schätze deine Antworten mit einem grünen oder roten Gesicht ein.

3 Let's find it!
1 Konntest du erkennen, um was es sich im Text handelt? ○ ○ → 1, 3a
2 Konntest du *keywords/phrases* erkennen und markieren? ○ ○ → 2a, 3b

4 Buckfast otters and butterflies
1 Konntest du wichtige *keywords* erkennen und markieren? ○ ○ → 2a, 3b
2 Konntest du mit Hilfe deiner *keywords* die Sätze in b) richtig kennzeichnen? ○ ○ → 2b
3 Konntest du mit Hilfe deiner *keywords* die Fragen in c) beantworten? ○ ○ → 3b

c) Wenn du dich rot eingeschätzt hast, schau dir die rechte Spalte an. Die Nummern führen dich zu den passenden Übungen im Skills Training (S. 54–55). Dort kannst du gezielt Leseverstehen trainieren.

1 Dos and don'ts ➜ SF 6, 9 (p. 85)

Look at the text quickly. What do you think it is about? Tick (✓) the correct picture.

TIP: Before you read, look at the **title** and **picture(s)**. From these you can often guess what the text is about.

Ponies have lived on Dartmoor since history began. They run freely on the moors, but they all have owners. Every year in autumn farmers sell some ponies. People like to buy them as riding ponies for children. They are small but strong. They look sweet, but remember that they are wild.

- Stay away. Don't try to get near them for photos – they sometimes kick or bite.
- You are not allowed to feed them. If visitors feed them, they stand near roads and wait for food from cars. But cars can kill or hurt them, and our food is not their food. It can make them very sick.
- Don't leave litter on the moors. If ponies eat plastic bags, they can die.

2 Dartmoor's history ➜ SF 6, 9, 11 (pp. 85–86)

a) Read the sentences in b) and mark keywords and phrases. Then read the text and mark the parts in the text where you find information about your keywords.

TIP: **Keywords** are often **nouns** and **verbs**. Mark words that tell you **who** did **what** or what happened **when**. **Key phrases** often tell you **when** (times), **where** (places) and **why** (reasons) something happened. **Names** and **numbers** are often important too.

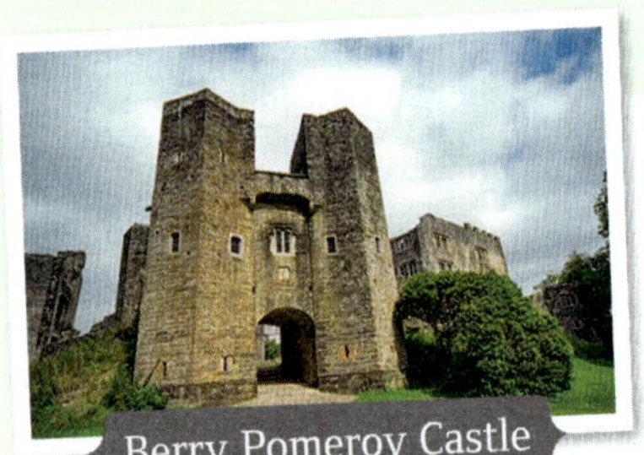

Berry Pomeroy Castle

Dartmoor is 295 million years old. Archaeologists have found some of the oldest houses and churches in England on Dartmoor, for example, Tavistock Abbey, from around the year 961.

Some of Devon's oldest castles are on Dartmoor. Castles are popular with tourists because they always have fascinating histories. The largest castle was at Okehampton. Today you can walk through its ruins and woods, or have a picnic by the river. You can also take an audio tour and listen to the castle's ghost stories! At the time of King Henry the Eighth, the Marquis of Exeter lived in the castle. But the marquis had problems with the king, so in 1538 he lost his head. But does his ghost still live there?

Berry Pomeroy Castle lies in a beautiful valley near Totnes. The prominent Pomeroy family began to build the castle in the late 15th century. But there wasn't enough money to finish it, so the Seymours became the new owners. Lady Jane Seymour became Henry the Eighth's third queen (he had six altogether!). People think that this is the most spooky[1] castle in Devon. They say that in the past, ghosts of the White Lady and the Blue Lady have appeared, both unhappy daughters of the Pomeroy family who died in the castle. Nobody really believes[2] these stories – but tourists like them!

b) Are the sentences right (R) wrong (W), or is the information not in the text (N)? Look at the parts in the text that you have marked.

1 Some of England's oldest buildings were on Dartmoor.
2 Okehampton was the largest castle.
3 There are no audio tours at Okehampton.
4 The Marquis of Exeter died in his sleep.
5 Berry Pomeroy Castle has the most visitors.
6 This castle also has the most ghost stories.
7 Five generations of Seymours lived here.
8 Tourists don't like ghost stories.

[1]spooky ['spu:ki] *gespenstisch, unheimlich* [2]believe [bɪ'li:v] *glauben*

3 Taking care ➜ SF 6, 9, 11 (pp. 85–86)

a) Look at the text quickly. Match the headings and the paragraphs. Write A–F in the boxes.

A Gates, not walls
B Fires
C Go prepared
D No souvenirs
E Driving[1]
F Stay in touch

When you go to Dartmoor, it is important to take care in all seasons and at all times.

1 Remember that the weather changes very quickly from sun to storm. Prepare for these changes. When it rains the ground quickly becomes wet and muddy. Wear strong walking boots. Take a rain jacket, a map, a torch, a mobile, enough food (maybe chocolate and nuts) and water. ☐

2 You see lots of stone walls around fields on Dartmoor. They are not only part of Dartmoor's history. They are important for the safety of farm animals and wildlife. Please do not jump or climb over the walls. They can fall down. Use the gates and remember to close them behind you. ☐

3 If you travel by car, remember that others use the roads too: walkers, riders, people on bikes, families with small children, ponies and farm animals. Wild animals often cross roads at night. Drive slowly. Never drive faster than 40 miles per hour. ☐

4 Dartmoor stones and rocks are not souvenirs. Please do not move them and do not take them home. Small animals often make their homes under stones and rocks. They are also important to archaeologists. ☐

5 If you are on the moors with friends or family, stay together. If you're alone, use a map and stay on the paths. Mists often appear on the hills and you can lose your way. Tell somebody where you are going and when you should be back. ☐

6 Camping and cooking on the moors is fun, but please be careful with cigarettes and campfires. Grass, trees and plants are often dry and can easily catch fire. Fires are dangerous in strong winds. They kill animals and take away their homes. If you see a wild fire, phone 999 and report it. ☐

TIP: You don't have to understand every **new word**. You can often guess a word from the **context**, from a **word you already know**, or from a **German word**. What do you think *safety* means?

b) Mark keywords in the questions. Use them to find the answers in the text. Write your answers to the questions in your exercise book.

1 The weather on Dartmoor often changes quickly. How can you prepare for that?
2 Why must you drive slowly on Dartmoor?
3 Why are stone walls important?
4 Why aren't visitors allowed to take home stones as souvenirs?
5 How can fires start? Why are fires on Dartmoor dangerous?

[1] drive [draɪv] *fahren*

Celebrate!

1 WORDS Lucy loves celebrations ➜ *SB (pp. 84–85)*

Finish what Lucy says with words from the box in the right form. Read the text first.

(to) blow out · candle · celebration · costume · crowd · (to) dress up · Eve · festival · flag · fireworks · (to) light · parade · (to) take part in

On Saturday there's going to be a big c e l e b r a t i o n in Plymouth: Lord Mayor's Day. There's the big _ _ _ _ _ _ which goes along Armada Way. People _ _ _ _ _ _ _ in colourful[1] _ _ _ _ _ _ _ _, and bands play. In the streets there are large _ _ _ _ _ _ of people with _ _ _ _ _. They clap and cheer. Then there's a great stage show with live music and dancing. My friends and I are going to _ _ _ _ _ _ _ _ _ _ it! There are lots of other _ _ _ _ _ _ _ _ _ in Plymouth, like the three-day food festival in August with lots of yummy food stalls! That's one of Dad's favourites. New Year's _ _ _ is cool too. We stay up late and watch the _ _ _ _ _ _ _ _ _ at midnight. There's a great view from the Hoe. Birthdays are good too. Mum always makes us a cool birthday cake with _ _ _ _ _ _ _, one for each year. Mum _ _ _ _ _ _ the candles and we _ _ _ _ them _ _ _ and make a wish. That's fun, but I have lots of wishes and not enough birthdays!

2 The show will be great (*will*-future: statements) ➜ *SB (p. 87)* • *GF 13 (p. 95)*

Sam and Lucy are talking about Lord Mayor's Day. Finish the students' dialogue with will or won't.

Sam: This will be my second Lord Mayor's Day in Plymouth, Lucy.

Lucy: I'm sure we ________ have a good time. But I think I ________ be nervous on stage.

Sam: That's silly. You ________ be nervous. You ________ be great.

Lucy: Well, I hope I ________ forget the words of the songs.

Sam: Well, nobody ________ know. So why worry?

Lucy: And I hope I ________ look silly in my costume.

Sam: Lucy, talk to Leo. He loves shows. He ________ be nervous. Maybe you ________ feel better then.

Lucy: I think all our parents and friends ________ come. I hope our show ________ be as good as last year.

Sam: Well, it ________ be as good as last year. It ________ be better than last year – because we ________ be in it!

[1] colourful ['kʌləfl] *bunt*

3 Maybe I'll be a teacher (*will*-future: statements) ➜ *SB (p. 87) • GF 13 (p. 95)*

When you're 28, what do you think your life will be like? Write five sentences.
You can use the ideas in the table or your own ideas. You can make funny sentences too.

		be	an interesting/boring job
		have	an actor/an artist/a farmer
Maybe	I'll	live in	French/Spanish/...
I'm sure	I won't	speak	married/single ...
I hope		work (in)	a different country/the UK/
		travel (to)	the USA/Africa/India/...
			(with) animals
			(with) children

1 *I'm sure I won't have a boring job. Maybe I'll have an elephant farm in Africa.*

2 ______

3 ______

4 ______

5 ______

6 ______

4 When will the party start? (*will*-future: questions) ➜ *SB (p. 87) • GF 13 (p. 95)*

Nina wants to go to Emily's party. Read Nina's answers and write her mum's questions. Begin with when/how/how many/who or with will and choose the correct verb: be (3 x), call, finish, get, *start*, take.

Mum	Nina
1 *When will Emily's party start?*	About six o'clock, Emily said.
2 *And* ______ ?	Not too late, at about ten.
3 ______ ?	About twelve kids will be there, I think.
4 ______ ?	Amira will be there, Charlotte too.
5 ______ at the party?	Yes, Mum. Of course there will be boys at the party.
6 ______ to Emily's house?	Yes, I'll take the bus with two others.
7 And ______ home too?	Yes, we'll get the bus home too.
8 ______ when you get on the bus?	Yes, I'll call you when we get on the bus. Then you or Dad can meet us.

5 My next birthday ➜ SB (p. 87) • SF 13 (p. 86)

In an email, an English friend asks you about your next birthday. Here is part of the email. Answer the questions. Write about a hundred words in your exercise book.

> I think it will be your birthday soon. Is that right? Tell me about it.
>
> How old will you be? How will you celebrate? Do you think you'll have a party? How many friends will you probably invite? What will you do with your friends? Will you have a birthday cake with candles? Will you have pizza and ice cream?
>
> …

On my next birthday I'll be … I (don't) think I'll/we'll …, maybe I'll …, I'll/We'll probably …, I'm sure I'll/I won't …

6 WORDS Clothes ➜ SB (p. 88)

a) ○ What are Nina and Dan wearing for Emily's party? Write the clothes words.

b) Write a short paragraph each about Nina's and Dan's clothes in your exercise book.

Today Nina/Dan is wearing … Her/His … is/are …

c) ● What are you wearing today? Write a paragraph in your exercise book.

7 In a clothes shop ➜ SB (p. 88) • SF 15 (p. 87)

Write a dialogue in a clothes shop. **A** wants to buy a pullover/T-shirt/jacket/… for a party. **B** is the shop assistant. First, put the phrases below into two lists, for speakers A and B. Then add more phrases and write the dialogue. Practise your dialogue with a partner and act it out in class.

Can I help you? I'm looking for…/I'd like … Have you got…? Just a moment, I'll look … How much is/are …? That's too expensive/small/… Which size/colour/design … Small, medium or large? I (don't) like this … Here's your change. I'll take this …

8 German Karneval
➜ SB (p. 88) • SF 12 (p. 86)

Your English cousin wants to know about German Karneval. You find this information. Answer your cousin's questions in English. First read the questions and mark important parts in the text.

Karneval ist ein tolles Volksfest, das einmal im Jahr gefeiert wird – ganz besonders in Städten im Rheingebiet wie Köln, Düsseldorf und Mainz. In Süddeutschland sagt man nicht Karneval, sondern Fastnacht oder Fasching dazu. In Norddeutschland ist der Straßenkarneval nicht so verbreitet. Die Karnevalszeit beginnt am 11. 11. und dauert bis ungefähr Mitte Februar. In dieser Zeit gibt es überall leckere Krapfen[1] (oder Berliner) zu kaufen.

Karnevalsumzüge gab es schon im 13. Jahrhundert. Damals wollten die Menschen den Winter vertreiben. Heutzutage ist der Höhepunkt am Rosenmontag[2]. Da gibt es die meisten Umzüge durch die Stadt. Schulkinder haben frei und die Geschäfte sind meist geschlossen. Lange Umzüge mit bunt geschmückten Wagen[3] und verkleideten Menschen ziehen stundenlang durch die Straßen. Auch Zuschauer verkleiden sich oder tragen Masken und jubeln den Wagen zu. Menschen wollen Spaß haben und feiern. Auch Kinder feiern viele Kostümpartys. Karneval ist bunt, laut und fröhlich. Am Mittwoch nach Rosenmontag ist dann alles vorbei – bis zum nächsten Jahr.

1 When does it take place?

____

____

2 How do people celebrate?

____

____

3 Are there special things to eat in the Karneval time?

____

____

4 Are there special activities for children?

____

____

9 EXTRA Festivals are fun, aren't they? (Question tags)
➜ SB (p. 88) • GF 14 (p. 95)

a) Finish the dialogue with the correct question tags.

Dan: Festivals are great fun, aren't they?

Nina: Sure, when it doesn't rain. It rained on Lord Mayor's Day last year, ______________?

Dan: I can't remember, but it won't rain this year, ______________?

Nina: Mum says it will be a bit rainy in the morning, but it will be sunny later.

Dan: Oh, well, we'll see. Leo is so excited. He can't wait for Saturday, ______________?

Nina: I know. He loves celebrations, ______________? But you like them too, ______________?

Dan: Yes, of course. It's better than Saturday shopping, ______________?

The parade starts at 1 o'clock, ______________?

Nina: Yes, that's right. We can all watch it together, ______________?

Dan: I'm not sure. At 1 o'clock Nick will probably still be busy at the food stalls, ______________?

b) 29 Think about how to say the question tags in a). Does your voice go up ↑ or down ↓? Listen and check.

[1] *Krapfen/Berliner* doughnut [ˈdəʊnʌt] [2] *Rosenmontag* Monday before Pancake Day [3] *(Karnevals)Wagen* float [fləʊt]

10 READING COURSE Taking notes
➜ SB (p. 89) • SF 10 (p. 86)

a) Read the text and take notes on a card or in your exercise book. Note only important facts in keywords, not full sentences. Use symbols, abbreviations and numbers. Important: who, what, when, where, why?

Notting Hill Carnival

West London's Notting Hill Carnival takes place every year on the last weekend (Saturday to Monday) in August. With 2 million visitors or more, it's one of the biggest street carnivals in Europe. If you like Caribbean[1] music, reggae, soul or hip hop and fantastic costume parades, this is the place to be.

The first Afro-Caribbean festival was in 1966, when immigrants in the Notting Hill area came together to celebrate, play music, sing and dance on the streets. The festival is now very popular. Every year there are fifty or more sound systems and bands, steel[2] bands and calypso bands and over a hundred floats[3] in the parades. The Carnival route is now

three and a half miles long. The streets are full of cheering crowds and wonderful aromas of delicious Caribbean food from the food stalls. Sunday is a great family day, the day of the Children's Parade, from 9 am to 7 pm. Even small children take part. They dress up in beautiful costumes and play in bands or dance. There are games and competitions with prizes for young musical talents. Don't miss the fun!

b) ● Check your notes. Are they clear? Will they help you to remember the most important information? Use them to prepare a short talk about Notting Hill Carnival for your class. Tell the class also why you would/wouldn't like to go to Notting Hill Carnival.

11 I'll help you after lunch (will-future, time phrases)
➜ SB (pp. 91–92) • GF 13 (p. 95)

a) Read the dialogues and finish B's sentences. Use a form of the will-future and time phrases. You can use words from the box.

ask · be · clean · do · get · go · ~~help~~ · practise

~~after lunch~~ · at the weekend · in a minute · next week · soon · this evening · tomorrow · when he gets home

1 **A:** My maths homework is too hard! **B:** Don't worry. I *'ll help* you *after lunch*.

2 **A:** This apple is brown inside.

B: Oh, sorry. I __________ you another one __________.

3 **A:** You promised to take the dog out this afternoon.

B: I'm too busy. I __________ it __________, OK?

4 **A:** It's so cold outside! **B:** Don't worry. It __________ summer __________.

5 **A:** I don't want to go to the cinema this week. **B:** OK, then we __________ instead.

6 **A:** Lucy told me the auditions are next week. **B:** Well, we __________, then.

7 **A:** What time is Grandma coming?

B: I don't know. I __________ Dad __________.

8 **A:** Has Nina cleaned my bike yet?

B: No. She's busy today, but she __________ it __________.

b) Act out the dialogues. Take turns to play A and B.

[1]Caribbean [kærɪˈbiːən] [2]steel [stiːl] *Stahl; hier: Steelband* [3]float [fləʊt] *Karnevalswagen*

12 If Mukesh comes, … (*if* or *when*) ➔ SB (p. 92)

a) ○ How do you translate if and when into German? Write **A** and **B** in the correct box:
A: falls, wenn **B**: dann, wenn, sobald

Maya: When Mukesh comes at two, I'll be free. ☐

Lucy: You mean *if* Mukesh comes at two, you'll be free. ☐

b) It will soon be Lord Mayor's Day. What are the students thinking? Finish the sentences with if or when.

1 ______ I don't go to Lucy's show, she'll be angry.

4 ______ I do the wrong dance steps, nobody will know.

2 What will happen ______ I forget the words on stage?

5 Everybody will clap and cheer ______ we do our kung fu demonstration.

3 ______ I go on stage, I won't be nervous.

6 Dad will be surprised ______ he sees my cool film of the festival.

13 WORDS Biker, drummer, … (Word building) ➔ SB (p. 92)

act · bike · dance · direct · drum · juggle · listen · play · run · shop · sing · speak · swim · travel · visit · win · write

a) ○ Make nouns from the verbs in the box.

+ -er	+ -r	+ l/m/n/p + -er	+ -or
listener	biker	drummer	actor

b) Finish the sentences with nouns from a).

1 The fire ______ does his show every weekend.
2 How many ______ are in the play?
3 The band's ______ plays very well.
4 Sam is good at basketball. He's a fast ______.
5 Maya is a good ______. She loves the Lido.
6 Leo is a great ______.
7 Justin would like to be a film ______.
8 How many ______ are there in Lucy's Rock Choir?
9 Lots of ______ come to the LMD celebrations.
10 The Broadway is full of ______ on Saturdays.

14 Sam's story

➔ SB (p. 92) • SF 6, 9, 11 (pp. 85–86)

a) Read the text.

It was the afternoon of the Lord Mayor's Day celebrations. Everyone was in town, the Bennetts too. "I love parades," said Sam, "And I'm really happy that our kung fu demonstration went so well." "Yes, you were all great," answered his mum. "But Sam, Dad and I have to leave now. Lily wants to stay with the parade, so you have to look after her. Don't lose her in the crowds! We'll see you at home at 5. OK?"

"But, Mum, that isn't fair. I'm going to meet my friends soon at the food stalls. Must I really have my little sister with me all day? Can't she go with you?" Sam asked.

"No, she can't. Be nicer to Lily, Sam. You know that we have to visit Aunt Cathy in hospital[1]. You can look after your little sister for an hour or two, can't you? OK? Now Lily, be a good girl for Sam. ☐ Bye!" "Hmm. Not my lucky day," thought Sam. He wasn't very happy, but he took Lily's hand. "Come on, little sis. Let's go for something to eat." ☐

"Hey, look, there's Maya. She's working at her dad's Indian food stall. Justin is there too. What about chicken[2] curry for lunch, Lily?" ☐

"But I don't want curry today. I want spaghetti, or chips like mum makes, then chocolate ice cream." "But Lily, there isn't a spaghetti stall here. The nearest place is Giovanni's, but we won't go there because I want to talk to my friends, here!" Lily was hungry – and angry with Sam.

"Hey, Justin! What did you think of our kung fu demonstration? I was cool, wasn't I? Did you see the move where I …?" "I'm hungry!" shouted Lily, but Sam was too busy with Justin and Maya. Suddenly, Lily pulled away from her brother and ran off into the crowd.

"Yes, Sam. You were cool. But wait, you were with Lily just now, weren't you? So where is she?" Sam looked around. There were people everywhere. "Lily! Lily!" ☐ he shouted, but the music was too loud.

"Oh, no! She's disappeared, Justin. Come on, we have to find her. I'm responsible for her. I can't tell Mum that I lost her … Mum and Dad will … Help me, Justin! Please!" ☐

"Sam! It isn't Justin. It's me! Get up! It's time for school. Mum had to go out early, so I have to wake you."

"Lily, you're here? I thought … Oh, Lily, I'm so happy to see you, little sister!" "Good! Then you can make me a big breakfast now!"

b) ○ Choose the best title. Tick (✓) a box.

☐ Sam's lucky day   ☐ At the food stall   ☐ A lesson[3] for Sam

c) Put the missing sentences in the right place in the text. Write a letter (A–E) in each box.

A You like chicken curry, don't you?

B Where are you?

C There will be some great food at the food stalls.

D For the first time in his life, Sam was really scared.

E Be sure to stay with him.

d) ● Find information in the text and finish the sentences in your own words.

1 Lots of people were in town because ____________________

2 Sam was responsible for Lily ____________________

3 Sam went to Maya's food stall with Lily, but Lily ____________________

4 When Lily disappeared, Sam ____________________

5 Sam was happy because ____________________

[1]hospital ['hɒspɪtl] *Krankenhaus* [2]chicken ['tʃɪkɪn] *Huhn* [3]lesson ['lesn] *hier: Lektion, Lehrstunde*

15 A UK music festival ➜ SB (p. 92) • SF 12 (p. 86)

● You read about *Music for Youth*[1] on the internet. Write notes in German in your exercise book so you can tell a friend about it. Explain:

- what *Music for Youth* is
- where and when the festivals take place
- what students do
- what students can learn.

Mark important parts in the text first.

MUSIC FOR YOUTH

MFY is a national charity for young musicians from across the UK. It organizes free festivals and concerts for thousands of talented music-makers from the age of 4 to 21. The national festivals take place in Birmingham and Scotland in June and July for six days every year. Students perform[2] in choirs, bands, orchestras or solo. There are workshops too, where they can learn a lot about different kinds of music: jazz, rock, pop and folk or classical music. Professional music mentors and teachers listen to their performances and help them to perform even better.

There are also regional festivals and concerts in many different places in the UK. The concerts give young musicians the chance to perform on stage in front of others. They take place in concert halls, music schools and town halls. Even very young children play instruments, sing and dance.

The first Music for Youth festival was in 1970. Since then, hundreds of thousands of young people have performed in music events and have shared their love of music.

16 STUDY SKILLS Presenting a photo ➜ SB (p. 93) • SF 18 (p. 87)

Prepare to present a photo to your group or class:

a) Match the phrases below to the four steps of presenting a photo. Write 1–4 in the boxes.

1 Introduce your photo.
2 Describe your photo.
3 Say what you think of the photo.
4 Finish your presentation.

	Step		Step
I chose the photo because …	3	Do you have any questions?	
I'd like to talk about this photo of …		I really like this photo because …	
Thank you for listening.		In the foreground/background you can see …	
I found this photo in a magazine/on the internet		I like the colours because …	
In the middle of the photo you can see …			

b) Find a photo or picture with the theme 'Festivals and celebrations'. You can choose a photo from this unit or find your own photo. Organize and prepare your presentation in your exercise book.

c) ● Talk about what your photo shows. Practise your presentation at home.

[1] youth [ju:θ] *Jugend* [2] perform [pəˈfɔ:m] *auftreten, vorführen*

17 PRONUNCIATION [f], [v], [w] ➜ SB (p. 96)

a) ○ 30 Listen and write the order of the words you hear. Write 1–10 in the correct boxes.

very	we	verse	ferry	few	wore	view	worse	V	four
☐	☐	☐	☐	☐	☐	☐	☐	☐	☐

b) 31 Listen and practise Morph's tongue-twisters alone and with a partner. Can you say them quickly and correctly?

1 Will Wilbur want to watch TV or an adventure DVD on Wednesday?

2 Fred wasn't very well when he visited Val and Victor in West Witton.

3 In winter there's a wonderful view of wild waves on the water.

4 It was very wet and windy when Will went to watch the fireworks in November.

18 What can we do? ➜ SB (p. 96) • SF 14 (pp. 86–87)

a) 32 Before you listen, look at the title and the pictures. What do you think Nina, Dan and their friends are talking about? ______

b) 32 Read the statements. Then listen again. Are sentences right (R), wrong (W) or is the information not mentioned (N)?

1 The kids want to raise money for the *Red Nose Day* charity. ☐

2 They will ask their teachers and families for ideas and help. ☐

3 The *Red Nose Day* motto is: "Be funny for money." ☐

4 Dan wants a schools football match in funny costumes. ☐

5 Emily and Amira think that's a good idea. ☐

6 Emily wants to make cakes and sell them at the youth centre. ☐

7 Amira thinks that a cake sale is a good idea. ☐

8 Amira would like a band evening or a karaoke evening. ☐

9 The quiz is Nina's idea. ☐

10 Dan and Nick will sell tickets for the quiz evening. ☐

19 My favourite festival ➜ SB (p. 96) • SF 13 (p. 86)

a) ● Write an article about one or more festivals in your area (about 100 words in your exercise book). Write about:

- when and how often the festival takes place
- how many people come to the celebrations
- how people celebrate (music, costumes, parades, food)
- why people celebrate (history, tradition)
- why you like the event(s).

One of the best festivals in our area is ... It takes place ... usually in August/... People like to ... There's ...

b) **EXTRA** Collect all the different texts and make a class magazine on celebrations.

20 Our favourite days ➜ SB (p. 96) • SF 12 (p. 86)

Nina and her friends tell you about other festivals in the UK. Tell your friends or partner in German 1) when each celebration takes place and 2) how people celebrate it.
First mark important facts, then take notes in your exercise book.

3

I like Halloween on 31st October. We sometimes have a party. You dress up in costumes as ghosts, witches and other scary things and you paint your face. It's fun when people don't know who you are. Mum has recipes for tasty Halloween party food too. Yummy chocolate spiders[3] and worms! We make a lantern with a face from a big orange pumpkin[4]. We light a candle inside it and it stands outside our house.

2

I like Valentine's Day on 14th February. You can send someone you like a card. Dad always gives Mum roses and chocolates. But it's more fun when you get a Valentine card and you don't know who sent it. Last year my brother Ranjiv was very surprised when he got a cool card without a name. He still doesn't know who sent it – but I know!

1

May Day is a nice old tradition too. It's on the first Monday in May. People celebrate the end of winter and the beginning of warmer weather. They put up a tall wooden maypole[1] in town and decorate it with flowers and colourful ribbons[2]. There's music and traditional dancing around it. It's a holiday, so there's no school or work. In our local park there are carousels, fun activities for kids and food stalls.

21 TEXT A day to celebrate ➜ SB (pp. 98–99) • SF 13 (p. 86)

a) ○ Read the text in your student's book on pp. 98–99 again. Circle the best title for parts 1 and 2 of the text.

Part 1: **A** Oh no, it's raining. **B** Singing and dancing in the rain **C** Leo's dance

Part 2: **A** Two mango lassis **B** Fun at the food stall **C** A great surprise for Maya

b) Now write your own titles for parts 3, 4 and 5.

Part 3: ____________ **Part 4:** ____________ **Part 5:** ____________

c) ● Finish the sentences with the correct information from the text. Use your own words.

1 In the morning, Lucy didn't feel great because ____________

____

2 Maya was very busy at the stall because ____________

____

3 When Lucy went onto the stage, ____________

____

4 John and Leo did an exciting trick. Leo ____________

____

d) ● Imagine you were at the Lord Mayor's Day celebrations in Plymouth. Write about your day in an email to an English friend (about 100 words in your exercise book). Use information from the text.
Write about:

- what you saw and heard
- who was with you
- the event you liked best
- what you had to eat and drink
- the weather
- how you felt

[1]maypole ['meɪpəʊl] *Maibaum* [2]ribbon ['rɪbən] *Band, Schleife* [3]spider ['spaɪdə] *Spinne* [4]pumpkin ['pʌmpkɪn] *Kürbis*

1 WORDS UK festivals

Finish the sentences with words from this unit.

1 On birthdays, it's tradition to have a birthday cake with __________, one for each year.

2 On Halloween, kids love to _____ ___ scary __________ and ______ their faces.

3 On Red Nose Day, people ______ money for _________.

4 On Lord Mayor's Day, children can _____ _____ in the children's ______ or in a show.

5 On Guy Fawkes Night, ________ of people __________ with __________ and bonfires.

2 I don't think I'll go to the parade (will-future)

Match the sentences 1–4 to the second part. Put I think or I don't think at the beginning of the second sentence.

1	It's raining.	[ ]	______	I'll go too.
2	I've already eaten enough.	[1]	I don't think	I'll go to the parade.
3	I'm hungry.	[ ]	______	I'll finish this Christmas cake.
4	Mum's going to a Diwali party.	[ ]	______	I'll have an apple.

3 Christmas in the UK

An English friend writes to you about Christmas in the UK and sends you photos. Answer your family's questions in German. Read the questions, mark important parts in the text and take notes in your exercise book.

1 Wie sieht ein *Christmas cake* aus?
2 Wann gibt es Geschenke?
3 Was sind *Christmas crackers*?
4 Was gibt es zu essen?
5 Was macht die Familie nach dem Mittagessen am 1. Weihnachtstag?

Christmas is a very special celebration. On the 24th, Christmas Eve, everybody is busy. Last year I helped Mum with the Christmas cake. It's a fruitcake with marzipan, white icing[1] and decorations – a Christmas tree, a Father Christmas or a snowman, for example. Our big Christmas tree looked great with its colourful decorations and white candles. We always put our presents for the family under the tree. In the evening, we often have visitors. We play Christmas songs and later we go to church.

Christmas Day is the main family day. On Christmas morning it's time for presents. What has Father Christmas brought? Kids get up very early. Everybody is excited. Well, maybe Dad isn't excited. He knows he'll get his hundredth pair of socks! Our grandparents always come to Christmas lunch. We decorate the table with candles and Christmas crackers. We pull the crackers before we eat. They go 'pop', and a paper hat, a small toy and a silly joke fall out. We put on the hats, of course. Everybody looks a bit silly, but that's OK. It's traditional. Do you have Christmas crackers in Germany? In the kitchen it smells fantastic. It's traditional to have a roast turkey with roast potatoes and vegetables, then Christmas pudding with vanilla sauce. We put holly and red berries (made of marzipan) on top. It looks cool, doesn't it? It tastes like a hot fruitcake. In the afternoon at 3 o'clock, everybody watches the Queen's speech on TV. Then we play with our presents or watch the Christmas circus on TV – and Grandpa falls asleep. Later there's tea with Christmas cake, but nobody is really hungry, so all our visitors for the next month get a large piece of Christmas cake. Is Christmas in Germany the same as in England? Write soon!

[1] icing ['aɪsɪŋ] *Zuckerguss*

4 A German celebration

Your English cousin is visiting you. In an email, a German friend invites you to a Volksfest[1]. Your cousin asks you some questions about what your friend has written. Read the questions below, mark important parts/key words in the text and answer the questions in English.

In unserer Gegend findet wieder ein großes Volksfest[1] statt. Wir feiern zweimal im Jahr. Es gibt ein Frühlingsfest im April oder Mai und ein Sommerfest im August oder September. Jedes Fest dauert 2 Wochen und jedes Mal kommen über 2 Millionen Besucher. Es gibt am Samstag einen großen Kinderumzug – ich bin auch dabei. Wir tragen Kostüme und ich spiele die große Trommel in der Band. Es gibt viele Attraktionen. Die „Wilde Maus" ist wirklich cool. Dann gibt es noch das Riesenrad, eine Achterbahn, viele tolle Fahrattraktionen, Losbuden, Souvenirstände, sogar eine Geisterbahn – nichts für mich!

Zum Essen gibt es tolle Sachen, Gerichte aus der Region und internationale Spezialitäten, indische oder afrikanische Küche, natürlich auch Imbissbuden, kandierte Äpfel. Es gibt auch viele Eisverkäufer – leckeres Eis!

Für Kinder gibt es auch lustige Sachen: Clowns, Jongleure, Wurfspiele, Karussells, und vieles mehr. Zum Abschluss des Festes gibt es ein großes Musikfeuerwerk. Habt Ihr Lust zu kommen? Wir könnten viel Spaß haben, oder? Anbei ein paar Fotos vom letzten Fest.

1 How often do people celebrate the festival? ______________________

2 How many people go there? ______________________

3 Will your friend take part? ______________________

____

4 What attractions[2] are there? ______________________

____

5 Will there be any food? ______________________

____

6 What is there for kids? ______________________

____

Check: Mediation

a) Vergleiche deine Antworten mit den Lösungen auf Seite 96 im Workbook.
b) Schätze dann deine Antworten mit einem grünen oder roten Gesicht ein.

	grün	rot	→
1 Konntest du in Aufgabe 3 wichtige Inhalte erkennen und markieren?	○	○	1 a, 3
2 Konntest du in Aufgabe 3 das Wichtigste sinngemäß auf Deutsch wiedergeben?	○	○	1 b
3 Hast du in Aufgabe 4 die wichtigsten *keywords/phrases* erkannt und markiert?	○	○	1 a, 3
4 Konntest du in Aufgabe 4 unbekannte Wörter auf Englisch erklären?	○	○	2
5 Konntest du in Aufgabe 4 die Fragen auf Englisch richtig beantworten?	○	○	4

c) Wenn du dich rot eingeschätzt hast, schau dir die rechte Spalte an. Die Nummern führen dich zu den passenden Übungen im Skills Training (S. 68–69). Dort kannst du gezielt Mediation trainieren.

[1] Volksfest *(people's) festival, fair* [feə] [2] attraction [ə'trækʃn] *Attraktion*

1 New Year's Eve in London ➜ SF 12 (p. 86)

a) You are in London on New Year's Eve with your family and you want to watch the fireworks. You see this poster. Mark the most important information to answer your family's questions in b). First read the questions.

London welcomes the New Year!

→ with a grand fireworks display at the London Eye, on the south bank of the Thames. It's fantastic – and it's free! After Big Ben strikes midnight, the fireworks begin. For at least ten minutes, you can watch a wonderful show of light and colour. But you won't be alone. Every year there are crowds of about a quarter of a million people from all over the world who want

to celebrate the big event. So get there early, even if it means a long wait! You have the best views from Westminster Bridge and the north bank of the Thames, opposite the London Eye. But you can see the display from most high buildings all across the city.

DON'T MISS IT!

TIP: Read the questions first. In the text mark only the **facts**[1]. Leave out[2] words and sentence parts that don't answer the questions.

TIP: Remember that **pictures** can help you to guess what you don't know. The picture shows you that the London Eye is a big wheel. You can guess words from the context too, for example 'bank': the north and south banks of a river must mean 'Ufer'.

b) Now answer your family's questions in German.

1 Wo findet das Feuerwerk statt? ____________________

2 Wie lange dauert es? ____________________

3 Wann sollten wir dort sein? ____________________

4 Wie viele Menschen werden dort sein? ____________________

5 Wo sieht man alles am besten? ____________________

____

2 Explaining words (Paraphrasing) ➜ GF 7 (pp. 91–92)

Here are some German words from exercises in this unit. Explain them in English.

TIP: These phrases can help:
It's a person/someone that …
It's a thing/something that …
It's a place/thing where (you can) …
It's like/similar to …
It's a kind of stall/ride/…

1 Eisverkäufer: *It's a person that sells ice cream at a (kind of) stall.*

2 Maske: ____________________

____

3 Achterbahn: ____________________

____

4 Losbude: ____________________

____

5 Imbissbude: ____________________

[1] facts [fækts] *Fakten* [2] leave out *auslassen*

3 Diwali[1] ➔ SF 12 (p. 86)

When you are in London, your friend Prita tells you about the Hindu festival of Diwali. Your family wants to know what Prita tells you. Read their questions below and mark the important parts in the text. Then answer the questions in German in your exercise book.

Every year in October or November we celebrate Diwali, the festival of lights, for five days. The fourth day is the start of the Hindu new year, and it's our most important festival. We decorate our homes and fill them with light, with oil lamps, colourful lanterns and candles. There are fireworks and bonfires, and always music and dancing. On Diwali Day we get up early. We visit family and friends and wish them 'Happy Diwali'. We eat special Indian food and wear our best traditional clothes. We make flower garlands[2] and give small presents of special Diwali sweets, fruits or candles. The story of Diwali celebrates how good triumphs over bad and how light triumphs over darkness. I think it's a nice festival.

1 Was bedeutet „Diwali" und wann wird es gefeiert?
2 Wie feiert man Diwali?
3 Welche Bedeutung hat das Fest?

TIP: You can often guess **words** from the context, a similar German word or from a part of a word you know. What do *decorate*, *oil*, *lanterns*, *triumph* and *darkness* mean?

4 Germany's biggest festival ➔ SF 11–12 (p. 86)

You are at the *Oktoberfest* in Munich with some visitors from England. You find some interesting information on a flyer. Tell your friends in English two facts each about: 1) visitors to the *Oktoberfest*, 2) how much visitors eat or drink, 3) what fun things you can do there, 4) *Oktoberfest* in other countries. Write in your exercise book. First mark important parts in the text.

Das Oktoberfest in Zahlen

Mit einer jährlichen Besucherzahl von 6–7 Millionen ist das Münchner Oktoberfest das größte Volksfest der Welt. Das erste Oktoberfest fand im Jahr 1810 statt, als Kronprinz Ludwig von Bayern heiratete. Wusstest du …?

Laut Statistik kommen 70 % der Besucher aus Bayern[3], 15 % aus anderen Teilen von Deutschland und 15 % aus Europa, USA, Australien und Japan. Während der 16 Festtage werden eine halbe Million Brathähnchen, 440 000 Würstchen und 25 Tonnen[4] Fisch verspeist. Über 7 Millionen Liter Bier[5], Tee, Kaffee und Wasser werden getrunken. Gäste werden von 1 600 Kellnerinnen und Kellnern bedient. Es gibt 80 Fahrgeschäfte. Zu den Favoriten gehören das Riesenrad und die größte mobile Achterbahn[6] der Welt! Sie hat fünf Loopings! Im Fundbüro liegen jedes Jahr ca. 4 000 Sachen, vor allem Brillen und Handys – und 35 000 Bierkrüge verschwinden jedes Jahr!

Das Fest ist so beliebt, dass es in anderen Ländern auch kleine Oktoberfeste gibt, z. B. in Cincinatti/Ohio, in China, Russland, Brasilien und Vietnam!

TIP: Make **short** sentences.
Say things **in a different way** with words you know. For example:

- 70 %: *seventy out of a hundred*
- eine halbe Million: *five hundred thousand*

You can use umbrella words like *food, meat, rides, countries*.

TIP: You can begin your sentences like this:
It says here … (Hier steht …)
There is/are …
Every year visitors/people/tourists come from …/They eat/drink/lose

[1]Diwali [diːˈwɑːli] [2]garlands [ˈgɑːləndz] *Girlanden* [3]Bavaria [bəˈveərɪə] [4]tonnes of … [ˈtʌnz əv] [5]litres of beer [ˈliːtəz əv bɪə] [6]roller coaster [ˈrəʊlə ˌkəʊstə]

A class trip

1 WORDS Sam talks about Tintagel ➜ *SB (p. 104)*

○ Finish what Sam says about Tintagel with words from the box.
Before you start, read the text.

bridge · cave · *cliffs* · defend · guide · legend · must · mustn't · narrow · needn't · path

Tintagel Castle is high up on the *cliffs* in North Cornwall. It has been famous for more than 800 years because people believe King Arthur lived there. Mr Petrock is a castle __________. He tells visitors about the __________ of King Arthur and about Merlin, the wizard who hid baby Arthur in a __________ because he was in danger[1]. The castle is a cool place for a class trip. We saw the main gate, which is very __________ so they could __________ the castle more easily. We climbed up a steep[2] __________ and we crossed a high __________ that takes you to another part of the castle on an island. You __________ wear special climbing boots for the visit, but you __________ be careful. And you really __________ fall off the bridge!

2 REVISION The day at Tintagel (Simple present) ➜ *SB (p. 105)* • *GF 2 (pp. 88–89)*

a) Finish the sentences with simple present forms.
Correct the wrong sentences.

1 The castle *doesn't have* (not have) a high bridge. *The castle has a high bridge.*

2 Mr Petrock __________ (work) with kids but he __________ (not be) a history teacher.

3 We __________ (know) what year Arthur was born. ____________________

4 The whole castle __________ (be) on an island. ____________________

5 Sam __________ (not want) to see Tintagel. ____________________

b) Write questions for Sam about Tintagel. Make questions with or without a question word.
Add more words if necessary.

scary/bridge/look? *Does the bridge look scary?*

lunch/can/eat/where/you? ____________________

King Arthur/legend/believe/of/you? ____________________

class trip/great/is/for/why/Tintagel? ____________________

[1] danger ['deɪndʒə] *Gefahr* [2] steep [stiːp] *steil*

3 REVISION What are they doing? (Present progressive: positive statements) ➜ SB (p. 107) • GF 4 (p. 90)

What are the students doing? Finish the sentences. Use the present progressive and other words you need.

1

At 11:15 they *are watching a film* in the visitor centre. (watch)

3

At 12 o' clock they ______________________ . (cross)

5

At 1:15 Lucy ______________ ______________ her mum. (phone)

2

At 11:30 Justin ______________ ______________ the castle gate. (film)

4

At 12:30 they ______________ ______________________ . (have)

6

At 3:30 the students ______________ ______________________ . (wait for)

4 REVISION Miss Bell's questions (Present progressive: questions) ➜ SB (p. 107) • GF 4 (p. 90)

a) Miss Bell wants to know what's happening on the bus home. Write her questions.

1 everybody – having – is – fun *Is everybody having fun?*

2 sitting – Justin – where – is ______________________

3 Lucy – about – telling – Sam – is – the snake ______________________

b) Write three more questions about the trip. Use the present progressive with or without a question word.

____

5 REVISION A message from Lucy (Simple present or present progressive) ➜ SB (p. 107) • GF 4 (p. 90)

Lucy phones her mum from Tintagel Castle and leaves a message.
Finish the sentences with verbs in the simple present or the present progressive.

Hi Mum! You haven't answered your phone, so I guess you *'re working* (work). I *am* (be) at Tintagel Castle. I ______________ (call) to say everything is fine. Right now we ______________ (be) outside. Some of the kids ______________ (finish) their lunch and Justin ______________ (film) the bridge. He always ______________ (film) our class trips! This afternoon we ______________ (not do) another tour … Oh, yes, I wanted to tell you that this afternoon we ______________ (leave) at half-past three. I'll be home just after five – the same time I usually ______________ (get) home on Mondays. See you later!

6 Why I like class trips ➔ SB (p. 107)

● Prepare to tell your partner what you like or don't like about class trips. Say why. First, make notes in your exercise book. Then use your notes to give a short talk. Here are some ideas:

> see and hear interesting things · can remember what you learn better · can be exciting/boring · do activities · have fun · ask lots of questions · get lots of information · take photos · long bus ride · do what the teacher says · stay with your group/teacher · listen to the guide · walk a long way · write a report

There are lots of reasons why I like/don't like class trips. First, .../ Second, .../Third, ... because ...
you needn't/mustn't ... you have to/don't have to ... you can/can't ...

7 WORDS Body words ➔ SB (p. 108)

a) ○ Write the answers in the puzzle.

1 It's the front part of your body above[1] your waist.
2 You have two feet and ten of these.
3 You need this to speak with.
4 Your teeth are in here.
5 You can put your rucksack or school bag on this.
6 It's between your head and your shoulders.
7 It's sometimes sore when you have a cold.

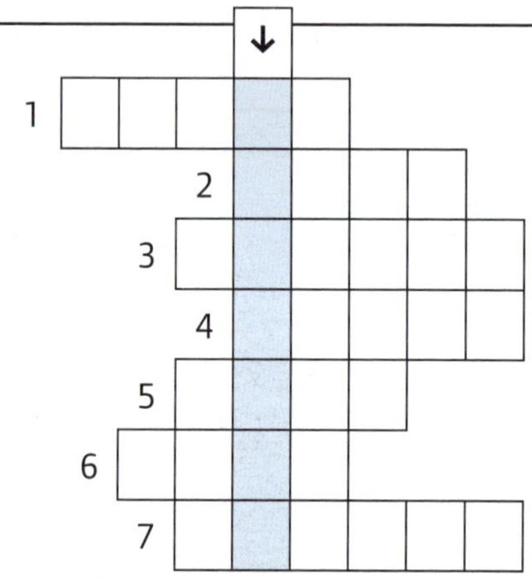

b) Finish the sentence with the word in the blue boxes:

➔ Justin groaned because his _ _ _ _ _ _ _ hurt.

8 Let's phone the doctor! ➔ SB (p. 108) • SF 12 (p. 86)

a) 33 Your English cousin, Ben, is staying with you. He feels ill. Your parents aren't at home, so you phone the doctor. Finish your part of the conversation in German or English. Then listen to the rest of the conversation and say your answers.

You: Guten Morgen, Frau Doktor. Hier spricht … Mein Cousin Ben aus England ist hier zu Besuch und es geht ihm nicht gut. Meine Eltern werden erst am Abend zu Hause sein.

Doctor: Aha. Was hat denn dein Cousin? Frag ihn bitte, was ihm genau fehlt.

You: *The doctor wants to know what's wrong with you.*

Ben: Well, I feel sick and my stomach hurts. I've been sick three times.

You: *Frau Doktor, ihm ist schlecht. Er* __________

Doctor: Was hat er denn heute gegessen?

You: What __________

Ben: Not much. Only toast and jam and a mug of cocoa for breakfast.
And you know that I wasn't hungry at lunchtime. I only had a bit of soup.

You: __________

Doctor: Wann haben die Magenschmerzen angefangen?

Listen and go on.

b) 34 Listen and check. Were your answers similar? Do this exercise at least twice.

[1]above [ə'bʌv] *über*

9 READING COURSE Using skills that you have learned ➜ SB (p. 109) • SF 11 (p. 86)

a) Scan the text in b) for the names of the characters. Mark them in the text.

b) Read the text. Then circle the best title.

A Arthur, boy and king **B** Arthur, the boy **C** Arthur becomes a knight

When King Uther was dying, Merlin asked him, "My king, is it your will that your son, Arthur, should become king after you?" Uther's last words to Merlin were, "My friend, it is my will and my command." Many lords and nobles[1] of the land were present when Uther died. They heard his last words with great surprise, because nobody knew that Uther had a child. Who was this son who should become king? Who was this Arthur? And where was he?

Uther was a good and strong king, but after his death there was fighting all over the country for many years. They were dangerous times. Lords and nobles became enemies. They formed armies[2] and fought against each other, even against their neighbours. They all wanted to become king.

Arthur lived with Sir Hector, his wife and son Kay in the country. Hector owned land and houses in the country and in London. They were kind to Arthur and they took care of him as if he was their own son. Arthur loved them too, as his parents. He was safe with his new family. He did not know that his true father was King Uther and that his mother was Queen Igraine – and Hector and his family did not know that Arthur was Uther's son.

Arthur grew up to become a good person. He was a clever, polite[3] child and a good-looking young boy. He worked hard in the castle and spent his free time riding and walking through the forests. He loved horses and was an excellent rider. When he was older, Merlin began to visit Arthur at Hector's castle and told him lots of things that a future king should know. Arthur did not understand why.

Arthur wanted to become a knight, like Kay, and Hector began to teach him all the skills that a knight needed. Arthur was a good student, brave too. He worked hard and he quickly learned how to use a sword and how to fight in a tournament[4]. He was not afraid of danger. When he was a young man, he became Sir Kay's squire[5] – and soon his life would change …

c) Scan the text for these words. Underline them and try to find their meanings in German, at first without a dictionary. Write them down.

- command Befehl
- nobles ____
- present ____
- army ____
- brave ____
- squire ____
- safe ____
- polite ____
- tournament ____

d) Take notes from the text which will help you to answer these questions in class.

1 What were Uther's last words? ____

2 Why was there fighting after Uther died? ____

3 Where did Arthur live as a boy? ____

4 Who was Kay? ____

5 How did Arthur spend his time as a young boy? ____

6 When did Merlin come back into his life? ____

e) 35 Listen to the text. Then read it aloud two or three times, clearly and slowly. Remember where to pause.

[1]nobles ['nəʊblz] [2]army ['ɑːmi] [3]polite [pə'laɪt] [4]tournament ['tʊənəmənt] [5]squire ['skwaɪə]

10 REVISION Maya's visit to Bath (Simple past) ➜ SB (p. 111) • GF 1 (p. 88)

Finish Maya's sentences. Put the underlined verbs into the simple past.

1 I usually go to Bath in December, to see my cousins, but this year I *went* in July.

2 The journey to Bath can take three hours sometimes, but this time it only ______ two hours.

3 I don't usually see a lot in Bath, but on this trip I ______ the fantastic Roman baths.

4 At school we always eat in the canteen, but in Bath we ______ our lunch in the park.

5 I didn't know Mrs Wilson could catch things quickly, but she ______ Lara's Frisbee easily.

6 I wanted to get a souvenir, but all I ______ was an ice cream!

11 WORDS A class trip ➜ SB (p. 107)

○ Find 30 words and phrases for a class trip.
Write them in three groups.

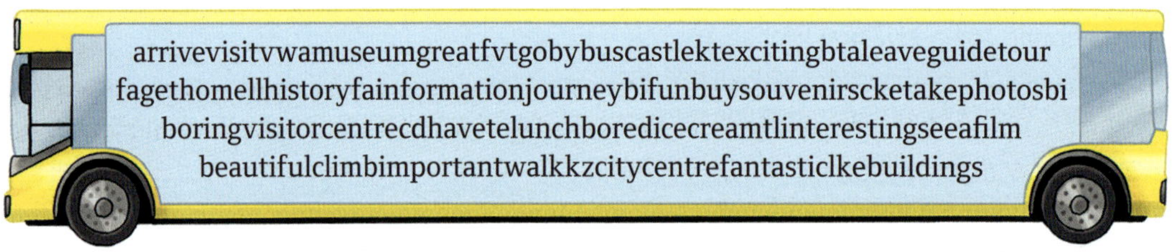

1 **Travel:** *arrive,* ______

2 **Things to see and do:** *visit a museum,* ______

______

3 **Describing your trip:** *great,* ______

12 An email ➜ SB (p. 111) • SF 13 (p. 86)

Imagine you are Sam or Lucy. Write an email to Abby about the class trip:
what you saw and did, where you went, what happened next. Use the simple past.
You can use words and ideas from exercise 11. Write about 80 words.

First/Then/After that ... In the afternoon, ... Later ... On the way home ...

Hi, Abby!

Yesterday we went on a class trip to Tintagel Castle in Cornwall. We left ...

______

______

______

______

______

13 Writing a report (the 5 Ws + *how*) ➜ *SB (p. 111) • SF 13 (p. 86)*

a) Read Nina's report about her last class trip.

Our class trip to Exeter
by Nina Hunt

On Tuesday, 3rd June our class, 8 AC, went on a trip to Exeter[1] by bus. Our class teacher and Mr Taylor, our history teacher, went with us. We are learning about the history of Devon and the south-west just now, so of course we had to visit Exeter, which is one of the oldest cities in England. In the morning, we took a walking tour of the city in two groups. I was in Mr Taylor's group. We had a Red Coat guide, who told us lots of interesting things about Exeter's past. He was funny too, so we all listened carefully. We saw part of the City Wall, which the Romans built. The Romans didn't get as far as Plymouth, so we don't have a city wall – I don't think. We saw St. Peter's Cathedral[2] and the Historic Quayside[3]. We went in the visitor centre there for some information and magazines. At lunchtime we had our sandwiches in a park. We saw some kids playing football, so we joined in. Mr Taylor told us a few history jokes. We didn't understand all of them – but we laughed anyway. The best joke was when Mr Taylor asked us, "Where is Hadrian's Wall[4]? Who knows?" One of the boys answered "Around Hadrian's garden?" In the afternoon we visited the RAMM in Queen Street, that's the Royal Albert Memorial Museum. It's a famous museum with 16 different galleries where you can learn about different times in history. We learned about how the Romans first came to Britain and what life was like for the Britons under Roman rule[5] about 2000 years ago. The Romans built towns, houses and good roads in many parts of the country – so they brought good things to Britain too. It was all very interesting. After that we looked round the museum shop and bought postcards or souvenirs. On the way back to the bus, our teachers bought ice creams for everybody and we talked about our day. We said what was good about the trip and what was not so good. Most of us knew Exeter only as a good place to shop or for the theatre, but now we know lots more about the city. Yes, we learned a lot and had fun. It was a great class trip.

b) Find answers to the 5 Ws (who, where, when, why, what) + how in Nina's report.

who? – Class 8AC ______________________

____

____

c) Nina forgot to use paragraphs. How many are there in her report? Mark the first word of each paragraph.

d) In your exercise book, write the beginning (a paragraph) of a report about your last class trip.

On Wednesday, 9th June ... Our last class trip was ...

14 PRONUNCIATION Consonants at the end of words ([d/t], [b/p], [g/k]) ➜ *SB (p. 112)*

a) 36 Listen and mark the words that you hear.

1 bored / bought	3 pig / pick	5 bag / back	7 kid / kit
2 plate / played	4 hard / heart	6 write / ride	8 lift / lived

b) 37 Listen and write the words that you hear.

1 ______ 3 ______ 5 ______ 7 ______

2 ______ 4 ______ 6 ______ 8 ______

[1]Exeter ['eksɪtə] *Devons Hauptstadt* [2]St Peter's Cathedral [seɪnt ... kə'θiːdrəl] [3]quayside ['kiːsaɪd] *Kai* [4]Hadrian's Wall ['heɪdriənz] *ein hoher Grenzbefestigungswall im Norden Englands, 120 km lang, vom römischen Kaiser Hadrian erbaut* [5]rule [ruːl] *Herrschaft*

15 REVISION Nick's weekend in London (*going to*-future) ➜ *SB (p. 112) • GF5 (p. 90)*

Finish the dialogue. Use the *going to*-future.

Dan: What *are you going to do* (you do) in London?

Nick: ________________ (I visit) my granny and maybe meet my cousins.

Dan: ________________ (you do) some sightseeing?

Nick: No, ________________ (I not go) into town.

________________ (I help) my granny.

Dan: Sounds like ________________ (you be) bored.

Nick: Oh yeah? And what ________________ (you do) this weekend? Something better?

Dan: Er, no. ________________ (I do) my homework!

16 REVISION Lena's visit to an English school (*going to*-future) ➜ *SB (p. 112) • GF5 (p. 90)*

Lena from Germany is going to visit her partner school in England and stay with Amira.
They skype before Lena leaves Germany. Read Amira's answers. Then complete Lena's questions.
Use the *going to*-future.

1 *Are you going to meet me* at the airport? — Yes, Mum and I are going to meet you there.

2 What ________________ on my first day? — We're going to have a little welcome party with the family.

3 When ________________ your friends? — You can meet them at school on Monday.

4 ________________ a school uniform? — Yes, Mum's going to get you a uniform tomorrow.

5 How ________________ know what size I need? — It's OK. I've told her your size.

6 ________________ to school with us? — No, my brother is going to go on a class trip to Spain.

7 When ________________ to London? — Er … my grandparents want to take us next weekend, I think.

17 Where I'd like to go and why ➜ *SB (p. 112) • SF13 (p. 86)*

Tell a friend in an email where you would like to go on your next class trip.
Think of an interesting place. What can you see and do there? How far is it?
Write about 100 words in your exercise book.

I'd like to go on a class trip to ... It would be a good place to visit because ... You can ... There's ...

[1]pirate ['paɪrət] *Pirat* [2]pub [pʌb] *Wirtshaus, Kneipe*

18 A great place to see ➜ SB (p. 112) • SF 14 (pp. 86–87)

a) 38 Before you listen, look at the title and the pictures.
What do you think Dan and his friends are talking about? Write a sentence:

____

b) 38 Read the statements. Listen again. Are the sentences right (R), wrong (W) or is the information not mentioned (N)?

1 Drake went to sea when he was only 13 years old. R

2 At the time, the countries of Spain and England were good friends.

3 Drake was the first English sailor who sailed round the world.

4 He sailed from Plymouth in his ship the *Golden Hind* in 1581.

5 The Queen made him a knight on his ship.

6 He bought Buckland Abbey, a big house near Plymouth.

7 Dan has been to Buckland Abbey.

8 Drake fought against the Spanish Armada in 1577.

9 Drake was on the Hoe when the Armada arrived.

10 There were more Spanish ships than English ships.

11 The Spanish ships were also better than the English ships.

12 Visitors to Buckland Abbey can see Drake's famous drum.

19 King Arthur and his magic sword ➜ SB (p. 112) • SF 17 (p. 87)

● Describe the scene. Say what is happening and use these phrases: at the top/bottom, in the middle, on the left/right, in the foreground/background. Write at least six sentences.

20 WORDS Opposites ➔ SB (p. 115)

a) ○ Find pairs of opposites and mark the words in the same colour. Then write the pairs.

_______ – _______ _______ – _______

_______ – _______ _______ – _______

_______ – _______ _______ – _______

_______ – _______ _______ – _______

b) Finish with word pairs from a).

1 Guards from the upper mainland courtyard _______ the castle when enemies _______.

2 Arthur _______ lots of fights. He didn't _______ because he had a magic sword called Excalibur.

3 Lady Guinevere became _______ Arthur's _______.

21 PLAY The sword in the stone ➔ SB (pp. 114–115) • SF 13 (p. 86)

a) ○ Read the play in your student's book on pp. 114–115 again. Put the sentences in the right order (1–5).

1 There's a sword in the old stone. How did it get there? ☐

2 Long live King Arthur! ☐

3 He is Uther Pendragon's son and the true king. ☐

4 We have lost the battle and our great king is dead. ☐

5 The winner of tomorrow's tournament will also be our new king. ☐

b) ● Tell the story of the play in a few sentences.

1 **Scene 1:** Merlin asks Hector to _______

2 **Scene 2:** Outside a church in London, Hector and Kay see a sword in a stone.

They try to _______

3 **Scene 3:** At the tournament, Kay sees that _______

____

4 **Scene 4:** Arthur sees the sword in the stone. He wants to take _______

____

5 **Scene 5:** Arthur comes back with the sword and Merlin says _______

____

c) ● Do you like the story of King Arthur? Why (not)? Write a few sentences in your exercise book.
Ideas: knights, battles, magic, Merlin, magic sword, lots of films and computer games about King Arthur

22 EXTRA Book quiz

a) What do you remember about your student's book? Mark the right answers.
You need the letters in brackets in part b).

1 In the holidays, Justin visited his dad in …
- New York. (G)
- Boston. (H)
- Chicago. (S)

2 Leo's family name is …
- Baxter. (R)
- Taylor. (U)
- Cooper. (A)

3 Who goes to boarding school now?
- Lucy (E)
- Maya (N)
- Abby (V)

4 Leo is a very good …
- singer. (N)
- dancer. (E)
- actor. (A)

5 Loch Lomond is in …
- England. (T)
- Scotland. (A)
- Wales. (Y)

6 Sam and Justin go to Radford Park to …
- take a boat ride. (S)
- meet Lucy and Maya. (N)
- make a kung fu film. (G)

7 Who rescues Sam from the lake?
- Lucy (H)
- Maya (R)
- Justin (S)

8 Who visits the farm on Dartmoor?
- Lucy and Leo (O)
- Lucy and Maya (U)
- Lucy, Maya, Sam and Justin (E)

9 Who falls in the mud?
- Sam (A)
- Justin (M)
- Lucy (L)

10 Lucy and Maya go out on the moor …
- to take photos. (I)
- to find a missing lamb. (T)
- to see wild goats. (M)

11 The juggler's name is …
- Josh. (D)
- Jack. (M)
- John. (S)

12 Guy Fawkes Night is on …
- 4th November. (A)
- 5th November. (U)
- 6th November. (E)

13 On Lord Mayor's Day, Lucy's show is at …
- 3 pm. (M)
- 10:30 am. (Y)
- 2 pm. (R)

14 Who built Tintagel Castle?
- King Arthur (S)
- King Henry III (H)
- Prince Richard (M)

15 Who was King Arthur's true father?
- Hector (O)
- Merlin (S)
- Uther (E)

16 Who plays Arthur in *The sword in the stone*?
- Justin (R)
- Sam (U)
- Leo (N)

b) Write the letters after your answers in the speech bubble below.
If your answers are correct, they give you Morph's message:

1 WORDS What's missing!

Write words from this unit in the correct form.

1 At Tintagel Castle, 8 EB's **g**__________ was Mr Petrock. He said that **P**__________ Richard **b**__________ the castle almost 800 years ago. The **g**__________ who **d**__________ the castle lived in the Upper Mainland Courtyard. From there they could see who wanted to **e**__________ the castle, friends or **e**__________.

2 Nina doesn't feel well today. She has a **c**__________ and a bad **c**__________. She has an awful **h**__________ and a **s**__________ **t**__________ too. Nina's mum thinks that maybe she has a **t**__________, so she gets the **t**__________.

2 Sam's dream (Present progressive and simple present)

Finish the text with verbs in the present progressive or simple present.

"This week, after the class trip to Tintagel, I've had the same dream almost every night. In my dream I *am walking* (walk) to the castle when I *see* (see) King Arthur. He __________ (ride) with Guinevere. The guards that __________ (stand) at the gate __________ (point) their swords at me. I __________ (be) really scared. In the castle, all the people __________ (wear) strange costumes, but I __________ (wear) my Plymstock uniform. In the lower courtyard, knights __________ (fight) with swords. In the big kitchen, a cook __________ (make) food – with a very big knife! So I __________ (run) away fast! What does the dream mean?!"

3 Two reports

Find three paragraphs for each report (A and B) and put them in the correct order: beginning, middle and end. Write 1–6 in the boxes below.

1 After a cream tea at Grandma's, we took Ringo for a walk. He's a cool dog, but he barks a lot. After the walk, it was time to go home. Dad drove. We had a nice day, but I was tired so I slept all the way.

2 On Saturday, my parents and I went to Bath for the day, in our new car. Mum drove. My grandparents live near Bath, so we visited them. Grandma made roast beef for lunch – yummy!

3 It was warm and sunny, so we walked for miles but we also took the Tube[1]. The Tower was great, but we had to queue. We took lots of photos of Big Ben, Westminster Abbey and Buckingham Palace, and we went on the London Eye! It was fantastic. We saw so much in just two days.

4 In the afternoon we went into town. Mum and Grandma wanted to go shopping, so Dad and I looked round the famous Roman Baths. It was OK, but I liked the Fashion Museum better. There are costumes and dresses from 1600.

5 We travelled back on Sunday evening. We got home quite late, but it was a brilliant weekend – and I learned a lot about the great city and its history.

6 Last Friday evening, our family went on a long week-end to London. We took the 6:15 train to Paddington. It was a surprise for Dad's birthday. We were all excited – Dad too.

Report A: ☐ ☐ ☐ Report B: ☐ ☐ ☐

[1]the Tube [tjuːb] *Londoner U-Bahn*

4 A great trip

Write a report about a trip with your family or friends (a visit to a museum, castle, street festival, etc.).
Give answers to the 5 Ws + how in your first sentences. Before you start, make notes in your exercise book.
Then write at least 120 words. Don't forget to give your report a title.

Check: Writing

a) Vergleiche deine Antworten mit den Lösungen auf Seite 96 im Workbook.
b) Schätze dann deine Antworten mit einem grünen oder roten Gesicht ein.

	☺	☹	
1 Hast du in Aufgabe 3 *beginning*, *middle* und *end* jeweils erkennen und richtig zuordnen können?	○	○	→ 3, 4, 6
2 Hast du in Aufgabe 4 hauptsächlich das *simple past* für deinen Bericht benutzt?	○	○	→ 1
3 Hast du in Aufgabe 4 am Anfang deines Berichts Informationen zu den *5 Ws* + *how* gegeben?	○	○	→ 2, 3
4 Hast du im Hauptteil deines Berichts einige Details über verschiedene Aktivitäten und Geschehnisse in einzelnen Absätzen geschildert?	○	○	→ 4
5 Konntest du in deinem Bericht kurze Sätze miteinander verbinden, z. B. mit *but*, *because*, *when*, *so* oder mit *who*, *that*, um deinen Schreibstil zu verbessern?	○	○	→ 5

c) Wenn du dich rot eingeschätzt hast, schau dir die rechte Spalte an.
Die Nummern führen dich zu den passenden Übungen im Skills Training (S. 82–83).
Dort kannst du gezielt Writing trainieren.

1 Dan's last holiday ➜ GF 1 (p. 88)

Finish Dan's text about his last family holiday.
Use the verbs in the box in the simple past.

buy · do · go · have · laugh · meet · see · speak · stop · travel · try · visit · write

TIP: Use the simple past (not the present perfect!) for most verbs in your report:
*Wir **sind** nach Italien **gefahren**.*
*= We **went** to Italy.*

Last year we __________ to Italy. First we __________ Rome. We __________ all the famous buildings and __________ a tour with a guide. I __________ postcards to my friends and we __________ a few souvenirs. After Rome we __________ to the coast by car. We __________ at a little village on the way and __________ a fantastic XL pizza! I __________ a nice Italian kid on the beach. He __________ English and he __________ to teach my sister and me some Italian. Oh dear! We all __________ a lot.

2 Starting a report ➜ SF 13 (p. 86)

a) A good report tells the reader about the **5 Ws + how** in the first two or three sentences. Copy the table into your exercise book. Then match the words and phrases in the box to the question words in your table.

Who?	What?	When?	Where?	Why?	How?
my mum and I	…	…	…	…	…

yesterday · in the car · *my mum and I* · went to Bath · visited my cousin · on our bikes · to Bristol zoo · last week · went on a trip · on my birthday · by bus/train · last summer · to go shopping · to the theatre · to see the sights · to Plymouth · with my class · to learn about Francis Drake · to get information for a project

b) Think of two more words or phrases for each of the **5 Ws + how** and add them to your table.

3 Using the 5 Ws ➜ SF 13 (p. 86)

Write the first paragraph of reports A and B below (two to four sentences each). Your paragraphs should give the reader quick information about who did what, when, where, why (and how if you wish). You can choose a different order. Ideas from exercise 2 can help you. Choose only one place/event for each report.

A: A report about a day trip to a place in your area (museum, castle, park, aquarium …)

Yesterday/Last week my dad/mum/ … ______________________________

____

____

B: A report about a visit to the cinema/theatre/a concert, a sports event or a birthday party …

____

____

____

4 Giving details ➔ SF 13 (p. 86)

In your exercise book, write the **middle** part of report A or B in exercise 3. Give details about what you (and others) saw and did, or what happened. This part usually has more than one paragraph. For example, you can write a paragraph about the morning/afternoon, about the different places you visited or things you did:

In the morning, we walked/visited/went to/took a bus to ...
After lunch, we decided to do a tour of ... There were lots of people outside ...
The next place we visited was ... On the next day when we ...

5 Making your text better ➔ SF 13 (p. 86)

TIP: One long sentence is often better than two short sentences. Join short sentences with **linking words** and **relative pronouns**.

a) Choose a linking word from the box and make one sentence out of two.

after · and · but · because · before · so · when

1 It was warm and sunny. We went in the sea every day.

It was warm and sunny and/so we went in the sea every day.

2 We couldn't play football on the beach. There were too many people.

____

3 My mum liked the hotel pool. I thought it was boring.

____

4 We met some nice German people. We were shopping in town.

____

TIP: Morph's steps
1 Give information about the **5 Ws** at the **beginning**.
2 Give **details** in the **middle** part. Use a new paragraph for different times of the day, places or activities.
3 At the **end**, write a short **general or personal statement** (one or two sentences).

b) Now use the word to join two sentences.

1 We usually had lunch at an Italian restaurant. It was near the beach.

____

2 I met some nice kids. They came from Leipzig in Germany.

____

3 We found a street market. It sold really cool clothes.

____

6 Finishing your report ➔ SF 13 (p. 86)

a) Tick (✓) three sentences that you could use for the end of a report about a trip.

- We had a great day out and I'd like to go there again. ☐
- We saw some famous sights and I learned a lot. ☐
- A boy on the bus was sick. ☐
- When it got dark, we went home. ☐
- It was a very interesting trip – and fun too. ☐
- I bought a nice T-shirt for my sister. ☐

b) Now write a report about a good **holiday** or **weekend**. Use the tips, ideas and words from exercises 1–6a. Make notes first, then write at least 120 words in your exercise book or on the computer.

SF 1 REVISION Learning vocabulary ➔ SB (pp. 145–146)

- Führe dein Vokabelheft, dein Vokabelverzeichnis oder deinen Karteikasten aus Klasse 5 weiter.
- Lerne immer 7–10 Vokabeln auf einmal.
- Lerne neue und wiederhole alte Vokabeln regelmäßig.
- Lerne die Vokabeln mit jemandem zusammen. Fragt euch gegenseitig ab.

Gut behalten kannst du Wortschatz besonders mit diesen Techniken:

- Gegensatzpaare bilden, z. B. *rainy – sunny, happy – sad*
- Wörter in Wortfamilien zusammenfassen, z. B. *(to) sing – singer – song*
- Wörter in Wortfeldern sammeln – dabei schreibst du alle Wörter unter Oberbegriffen *(umbrella words)* auf.

Finde heraus, welcher Lernertyp du bist. Wie kannst du am besten Vokabeln lernen? Durch Hören, durch Bilder, am Computer (z. B. mit deinem e-Workbook) oder indem du dir eine eigene Geschichte um die neuen Vokabeln ausdenkst? Nutze diese Techniken häufig.

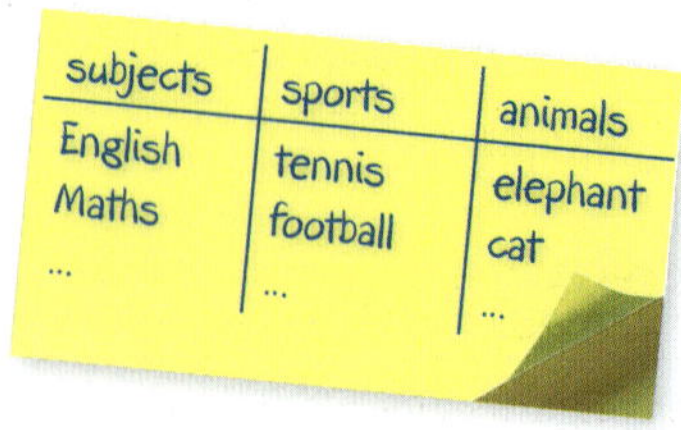

SF 2 REVISION Mind maps ➔ SB (p. 146)

- Schreibe das Thema in die Mitte eines leeren Blattes.
- Überlege dir Oberbegriffe zu deiner Sammlung von Ideen. Verwende unterschiedliche Farben für diese Hauptäste.
- Ergänze jede Idee, die zu einem Oberbegriff passt, auf einem Nebenast. Nimm dafür nur Schlüsselwörter. Du kannst statt Wörtern auch Symbole verwenden und Bilder ergänzen.

SF 3 Vocabulary picture poster ➔ SB (p. 146)

Vokabelposter können dir helfen, Wortschatz zu bestimmten Wortfeldern bildhaft zu veranschaulichen, damit du ihn dir besser merken kannst.

- Sammle Vokabeln zu deinem Wortfeld, z. B. in einer Mindmap, einer Tabelle oder in einer Liste.
- Überlege, welches Bild dir zu einem Wortfeld einfällt, z. B. ein Instrument zum Thema *music* oder der Umriss einer Landkarte für geografische Begriffe. Dieses Bild kann den Rahmen für dein Poster bilden.
- Zeichne dein Bild groß auf ein Poster und schreibe alle Wörter, die dir zu dem Wortfeld einfallen, in das Bild. Schreibe groß und gut leserlich.
- Hänge dein Poster an die Wand in deinem Zimmer oder präsentiere es in deiner Klasse.

SF 4 Study posters ➔ SB (p. 147)

- Schreibe wichtige Informationen zu deinem Thema auf.
- Suche alle Informationen heraus, die du auf dem Poster darstellen willst.
- Überlege, wie du das, was du dir merken willst, am besten darstellen kannst. Du kannst z. B. Kästen oder Tabellen verwenden.
- Finde einen guten Titel für dein Plakat.
- Gestalte dein Plakat. Schreibe groß und gut leserlich.
- Hebe wichtige Punkte hervor, z. B. durch Unterstreichen oder durch unterschiedliche Farben. Verwende aber nicht zu viele verschiedene Farben – sonst wird dein Lernposter unübersichtlich.
- Wenn du ein Lernposter zu einer Grammatikregel machst, kannst du auch ein paar Beispielsätze aufschreiben.
- Häng dein Poster zu Hause oder in der Schule an einer Stelle auf, an der du es häufig siehst.

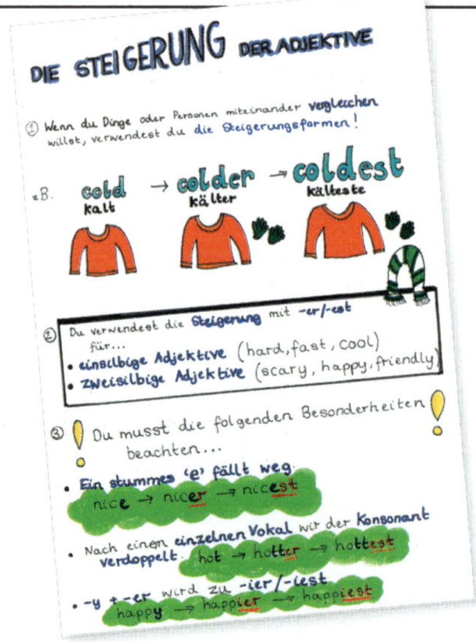

[1] in a nutshell ['nʌtʃel] *in aller Kürze, kurz und bündig*

SF 5 Making notes with a crib sheet ➔ *SB (p. 147)*

Sei ruhig kreativ. Dein Spickzettel ist nur für dich – wichtig ist, dass **du** verstehst, was du notiert hast. Diese Tipps können dir dabei helfen:

- Verwende nur ein kleines Blatt Papier.
- Schreibe keine ganzen Sätze, sondern verwende immer nur Stichwörter.
- Du kannst Symbole und kleine Zeichnungen verwenden, um den Text so knapp wie möglich zu gestalten. Verwende zum Beispiel:
  - "+" für "and"
  - Smileys für Gefühle, Flaggen für Länder, Strichzeichnungen für Dinge und Personen, über die du schreiben oder sprechen möchtest,
  - Pfeile für Richtungen oder Ortsangaben, eine Sonne für Tag/gutes Wetter usw.
- Arrangiere alles so auf deinem Spickzettel, dass die Reihenfolge der Ereignisse, über die du berichtest, deutlich erkennbar ist.

SF 6 REVISION Understanding new words ➔ *SB (p. 148)*

Unbekannte Wörter im Wörterbuch nachzuschlagen kostet Zeit und mindert auf Dauer die Freude am Lesen. Du kannst unbekannte Wörter oft auch ohne Wörterbuch verstehen, wenn du diese Hinweise beachtest:

- Viele englische Wörter werden ähnlich wie im Deutschen geschrieben oder klingen ähnlich, z. B. *discussion, statue, insect*. Ihre Bedeutung kannst du leicht erschließen.
- Du kannst englische Wörter auch verstehen, weil sie einem Wort aus einer anderen Sprache ähnlich sind, z. B. *voice (French: voix; Latin: vox)*.
- In manchen unbekannten Wörtern stecken bekannte Teile, z. B. ***sun**shine*, ***bottle open**er*.
- Bilder zum Text zeigen oft Dinge, die du im Text vielleicht nicht verstehst. Schau dir deshalb vor dem Lesen alle Bilder genau an.
- Wörter im Umfeld des unbekannten Wortes können dir helfen, die Bedeutung zu erschließen, z. B. *Let's hurry. The train **departs** in ten minutes.*
- Manchmal gibt es in einem der nächsten Sätze ein Wort mit der gleichen Bedeutung wie das, was du nicht verstehst, z. B. *He picked up a **pebble**. The small stone was red and black.*

SF 8 Reading aloud ➔ *SB (p. 149)*

- Stelle sicher, dass du den Inhalt des Textes gut verstanden hast. Kannst du Fragen dazu beantworten? Was passiert wem, wann, wo und warum?
- Überlege, was die Personen im Text fühlen. Sind sie fröhlich? Traurig? Ängstlich? Aufgeregt? Wenn du einen Text gut laut vorlesen willst, solltest du versuchen, diese Gefühle mit deiner Stimme und deiner Körpersprache wiederzugeben.
- Sieh dir die Satzzeichen gut an – sie zeigen dir, wo du Pausen machen oder deine Stimme verändern solltest. Bei einer Frage z. B. geht deine Stimme am Ende oft nach oben, und Kommas und Punkte zeigen dir, wo du eine sinnvolle Pause machen kannst. Es kann hilfreich sein, diese Stellen im Text zu markieren.
- Bevor du einen Text laut vorliest, übe das Lesen leise für dich, bis du ihn möglichst flüssig lesen kannst.

SF 9 Scanning ➔ *SB (p. 149)*

- Bevor du auf den Text schaust, überlege dir mögliche *keywords*, nach denen du suchen könntest. Es kann helfen, wenn du sie aufschreibst.
- Stell dir dann die *keywords* gut vor und geh mit deinen Augen sehr schnell durch den Text. Die gesuchten Wörter werden dir sofort „ins Auge springen".
- Du kannst auch mit dem Finger in breiten Bewegungen wie bei einem „S" von oben bis unten durch den Text gehen. Wenn du deine *keywords* gefunden hast, lies dort weiter, um Näheres zu erfahren.

SF 10 REVISION Taking notes ➜ SB (p. 150)

In Texten oder Gesprächen gibt es immer wichtige und unwichtige Wörter. Die wichtigen Wörter sind sogenannte Schlüsselwörter *(keywords)*, und nur die solltest du notieren. Meist sind das Substantive und Verben, manchmal auch Adjektive oder Zahlen. Folgende Punkte können dir auch helfen:

- Verwende Ziffern (z. B. „7" statt „seven").
- Verwende Symbole und Abkürzungen, z. B. ✓ („yes") und + („and"). Am besten erfindest du eigene Symbole.
- Bei Verneinungen verwende „not" oder streiche Wörter durch.

SF 11 Marking up a text ➜ SB (p. 150)

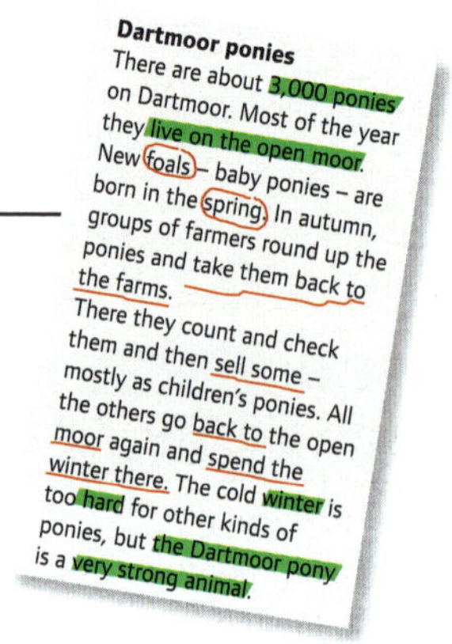
Dartmoor ponies
There are about 3,000 ponies on Dartmoor. Most of the year they live on the open moor. New foals – baby ponies – are born in the spring. In autumn, groups of farmers round up the ponies and take them back to the farms. There they count and check them and then sell some – mostly as children's ponies. All the others go back to the open moor again and spend the winter there. The cold winter is too hard for other kinds of ponies, but the Dartmoor pony is a very strong animal.

- Lies dir die Aufgabe genau durch.
- Lies den Text und markiere nur Informationen, die für deine Aufgabe wichtig sind. Nicht jeder Satz enthält Wichtiges, und oft reicht es aus, nur ein oder zwei Wörter in einem Satz zu markieren.
- Hebe wichtige Informationen hervor, z. B. durch Unterstreichen, Einkreisen oder Markieren mit einem Textmarker.
- Wichtig: Markiere nur auf Fotokopien von Texten oder in deinen eigenen Büchern.

SF 12 REVISION Mediation ➜ SB (p. 151)

Übersetze nicht alles wörtlich und gib nur das Wesentliche wieder. Du kannst Unwichtiges weglassen und Sätze umformulieren.

SF 13 Writing ➜ SB (pp. 151–152)

- Wenn du einen Text schreibst, in dem du eigene Gedanken darstellst, kann es hilfreich sein, wenn du dir vorher ein paar Notizen machst.
- Dein Text sollte aus drei Teilen bestehen: einer Einleitung, einem Hauptteil und einem Schluss. Diese drei Teile sollten klar erkennbar sein. Den Hauptteil kannst du unterteilen: jeder Abschnitt enthält eine neue Idee oder einen neuen Aspekt des Themas, über das du schreibst.
- Schreibe nie aus Vorlagen ab, sondern verwende immer deine eigenen Worte.
- Dein Text wird interessanter, wenn du Adjektive oder Adverbien verwendest, um Dinge, Handlungen oder Personen näher zu beschreiben.
- Wenn du fertig bist, dann lies deinen Text noch einmal gründlich durch und kontrolliere ihn auf Fehler. Oder lass deinen Text von einem Partner/einer Partnerin checken.

SF 14 REVISION Listening ➜ SB (p. 152)

Was mache ich vor dem Hören?

- Schau dir die Aufgabenstellung genau an. Was sollst du heraushören?
- Oft findest du zum Text Überschriften und Bilder, die schon einige Fragen beantworten: Wer spricht mit wem, wo sind sie, worüber reden sie?
- Überlege, was du selbst zum Thema schon weißt und welche englischen Begriffe im Gespräch fallen könnten.

Worauf sollte ich während des Hörens achten?

- Lass dich nicht verwirren, wenn es mehrere Sprecher gibt. Versuche dann, die jeweiligen Stimmen einer Person zuzuordnen.
- Wie reden die Menschen miteinander? Gibt es einen, der den Ton angibt, oder einen, der besonders ärgerlich oder traurig klingt?
- Höre gezielt auf die Hintergrundgeräusche – findet das Gespräch z. B. am Strand, auf der Straße oder in der Schule statt?
- Einiges wirst du nicht verstehen – keine Sorge, das ist nicht schlimm. Wichtiger ist, was du alles verstanden hast. Oft ergibt sich dann der Rest.

Und nach dem Hören?

- Wenn möglich, vergleiche mit einem Partner/einer Partnerin, was ihr verstanden habt.
- Wenn du einen Text ein zweites Mal hören darfst, notiere dir nach dem ersten Hören kurz, worauf du beim zweiten Hören besonders achten willst.
- Oft hilft schlaues Raten und Kombinieren.

SF 15 Speaking ➜ SB (p. 153)

Wenn du dich freundlich auf Englisch unterhalten willst, können dir diese Hinweise helfen:

1 Eröffne das Gespräch mit einer freundlichen Anrede oder Frage.
2 Wenn du etwas gefragt wirst, antworte nicht nur mit einem Wort.
3 Stelle deinem Gesprächspartner/deiner Gesprächspartnerin ein paar freundliche/interessierte Fragen.
4 Erzähle auch etwas von dir. Das hält das Gespräch am Laufen.
5 Verabschiede dich am Ende freundlich.

SF 16 REVISION Giving a presentation ➜ SB (p. 154)

Vorbereitung

- Sammle Informationen zu deinem Thema.
- Wähle eine Form der Präsentation aus, die das Thema gut veranschaulicht (Poster, Folie, Tafel, …).
- Mach dir Notizen, z. B. auf nummerierten Karteikarten.
- Bereite deine Medien vor (Poster, Folie, Tafelanschrieb, …).
- Übe deine Präsentation zu Hause vor einem Spiegel oder vor einem kleinen Publikum (Eltern, Großeltern, Freunde).
- Sprich laut, deutlich und langsam.

Durchführung

- Warte, bis es ruhig ist. Schau die Zuhörer/innen an.
- Erkläre, worüber du sprechen wirst und wie deine Präsentation aufgebaut ist.
- Lies nicht von deinen Karten ab, sondern sprich möglichst frei.

Schluss

- Sage, dass du zum Ende kommst und bedanke dich fürs Zuhören.
- Frag die Zuhörer/innen, ob sie Fragen haben.

SF 17 Describing pictures ➜ SB (p. 154)

Was?

- Sage zuerst, was du beschreiben willst: *a photo* · *a poster* · *a drawing*

Wo?

- Um zu sagen, wo etwas abgebildet ist, benutze: *at the top/bottom* · *in the foreground/ background* · *in the middle* · *on the left/right*
- Du kannst die Redemittel auch kombinieren: *at the bottom on the left* · *at the top on the right*
- Diese Präpositionen sind auch hilfreich: *behind* · *between* · *in front of* · *next to* · *under* · *over*

Wie?

- Geh bei der Beschreibung in einer bestimmten Reihenfolge vor, z. B. von links nach rechts, von oben nach unten oder vom Vordergrund zum Hintergrund.

SF 18 Presenting a photo ➜ SB (p. 155)

1 Stelle das Foto vor und sage, woher es kommt.
2 Beschreibe das Foto *(SF 17: Describing pictures)*.
3 Sage, was dir an dem Foto gefällt oder nicht. Wenn es eine Geschichte zu dem Foto gibt, erzähle sie.
4 Bedanke dich am Ende für die Aufmerksamkeit und frage, ob noch jemand Fragen hat.

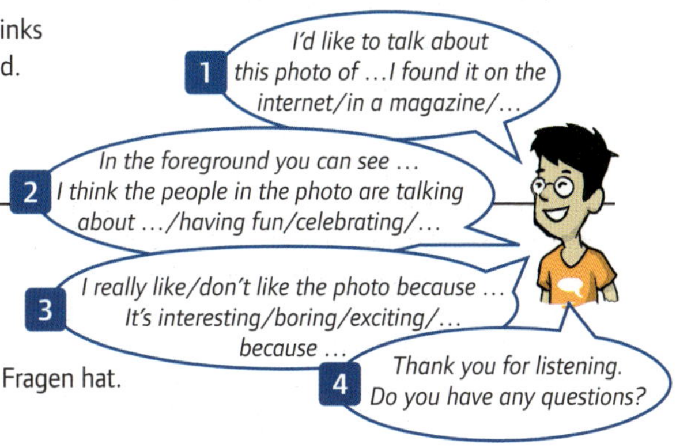

GF 1 REVISION The simple past ➜ SB (pp. 157–158)

a) Positive statements

*We **went** to Spain last year. We **stayed** in a nice hotel in Madrid and **visited** lots of museums.*

stay → ***stayed*** [steɪd] ***film*** → ***filmed*** [fɪlmd]
talk → ***talked*** [tɔːkt] ***watch*** → ***watched*** [wɒtʃt]

1 *It was rainy when we **arrived**.*
2 *Later the rain **stopped**, and it was warm and sunny.*

3 *We **tried** to do some sport, but it was too hot.*
4 *So we **visited** lots of museums.*
*I really **needed** that holiday.*

	Infinitiv:
*Justin **went** to the USA last summer.*	***go***
*He **got** back two days ago.*	***get***
*Sam and his dad **had** a race.*	***have***
*Abby **met** a German girl at her hotel.*	***meet***
*Sam **took** photos of sand sculptures.*	***take***

Mit dem *simple past* kannst du über **Vergangenes** berichten. Das *simple past* steht häufig mit Zeitangaben wie ***last year, yesterday, two days ago, in 2010***.

Bei **regelmäßigen** Verben hängst du ***-ed*** an den Infinitiv, um das *simple past* zu bilden. Es gibt für alle Personen nur eine Form.

! Beachte folgende Besonderheiten:
1 Ein stummes ***e*** fällt weg: ***arrive*** → ***arrived***
2 Nach einem einzelnen, betonten Vokal wird der Konsonant verdoppelt: ***stop*** → ***stopped***
3 Ein ***y*** nach Konsonant wird zu ***-ied***: ***try*** → ***tried***
4 Nach ***t*** und ***d*** wird die ***ed***-Endung [ɪd] ausgesprochen: ***visited*** ['vɪzɪtɪd], ***needed*** ['niːdɪd]

Unregelmäßige Verben haben eine eigene Form für das *simple past*, die du einzeln lernen musst.

Links findest du einige Beispiele.

➜ Liste der unregelmäßigen Verben, Schülerbuch S. 248–249

b) Negative statements

*Abby **didn't go** sailing with Tim – she went alone.*
*Sam's dad **didn't win** the race because he crashed.*
*Sam **didn't want** to leave a message for Justin.*

Eine Aussage im *simple past* **verneinst** du immer mit ***didn't*** + **Infinitiv** (Langform: *did not*).

Vergleiche: *Abby **went** sailing alone.*
*She **didn't go** with Tim.*
(nicht: *She didn't ~~went~~ with Tim.*)

Dies gilt für regelmäßige und für unregelmäßige Verben.

c) Yes/No questions and short answers

***Did** Maya **visit** Lucy's grandparents? – Yes, she **did**.*
***Did** you **go** on holiday in the summer?*
*– Yes, I **did**./No, I **didn't**.*
Sam: *Justin, **did** you **see** the Empire State Building?*
Justin: *No, I **didn't**.*

Fragen im *simple past* bildest du immer mit **did**.

Vergleiche: *Maya **visited** Lucy's grandparents.*
***Did** Abby **visit** Lucy's grandparents?*
(nicht: *Did Abby visit~~ed~~ Lucy's grandparents?*)

Dies gilt für regelmäßige und für unregelmäßige Verben.

d) Questions with question words

***What did** Sam **do** when it was cloudy and cold?*
– He went to the pier.
***Where did** Sam **take** the photo of the sand sculptures?*
– In Weston-super-Mare.
***When did** Justin **get** back? – Two days ago.*

Fragen mit Fragewörtern *(What, Where, When, Why, How)* bildest du wie Entscheidungsfragen.
Das Fragewort steht am Anfang der Frage, vor *did*.
Vergleiche:
*Abby **went** sailing.*
Entscheidungsfrage: ***Did** Abby **go** sailing?*
Frage mit Fragewort: ***When did** Abby **go** sailing?*

Die einfache Form der Vergangenheit

Bejahte Aussagen	Verneinte Aussagen	Fragen
I/You/He/She/It visit**ed** …	I/You/He/She/It **didn't** visit …	**Did** I/you/he/she/it visit …?
We/You/They visit**ed** …	We/You/They **didn't** visit …	**Did** we/you/they visit …?

GF 2 REVISION The simple present ➜ SB (pp. 159–160)

a) Positive statements

*I **get up** at 6:30 every morning. Then I **have** breakfast. After breakfast, I **go** to school. I usually **take** the bus. Maya **lives** in Plymouth. She **goes** to Coombe Dean School. She often **goes** sailing at weekends.*

Wenn du darüber redest, was **regelmäßig** (jeden Tag, immer, oft, meistens) oder **nie** geschieht, dann verwendest du das *simple present*.
In *simple present*-Sätzen stehen daher häufig
– die Wörter ***always, usually, often, sometimes, never***
– Zeitangaben wie ***every day, on Sundays, at weekends***.

*Lots of children **like** ice cream.*
*Dogs **eat** meat.*

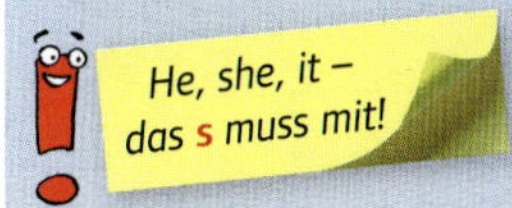

*I/You/We/They **like** dogs.*
He/She/It ***likes*** dogs.

Man verwendet das *simple present* auch, um allgemeine Aussagen zu machen.
Verben im *simple present* haben bei ***I***, ***you***, ***we*** und ***they*** keine Endung. Nur bei ***he***, ***she*** und ***it*** (der 3. Person Singular) wird ein **s** angefügt.

---

b) 3rd person singular: pronunciation and spelling

1 [s] *My dog **eats** lots of meat.* [-ts]
*And she **barks** a lot.* [-ks]

2 [z] *Morph often **hides** in the library.* [-dz]
*Dad always **comes** home late.* [-mz]
*Leo **knows** Lucy.* [-əʊz]

3 [ɪz] *Sue often **misses** the bus.* [-sɪz]
*Paul **watches** TV at weekends.* [-tʃɪz]
*Our teacher **uses** red pens.* [-zɪz]

*(to) **hurry up** – He's late for school, so he **hurries** up.*
*(to) **try** – Sam always **tries** to help his sister.*
*to) **play** – John **plays** football every Saturday.*

Der Laut **vor** dem **s** bestimmt die Aussprache.

1 Nach **stimmlosen Konsonanten**: [s]
Stimmlose Konsonanten sind z. B. [t], [k], [p], [f].

2 Nach **stimmhaften Konsonanten** und **Vokalen**: [z]
Stimmhafte Konsonanten sind z. B. [d], [b], [g], [v], [m].

3 Nach **Zischlauten**: [ɪz]
Zischlaute sind z. B. [s], [z], [ʃ], [tʃ], [dʒ].
Nach Zischlauten wird *es* oder *s* angehängt, je nach Schreibung des Infinitivs: *miss – misses* • *use – uses*.

Bei Verben, die auf **Konsonant + y** enden, gibt es eine Besonderheit in der 3. Person Singular: ***y + s → ies***.
Aber **Vokal + y** bleibt unverändert: ***play + s → plays***.

---

c) Negative statements

*I/You/We/They **don't** **live** in Britain.*
He/She/It ***doesn't live*** in Britain.

Eine Aussage im *simple present* **verneinst** du

- bei *I, you, we, they* mit ***don't* + Infinitiv**
- bei *he, she, it* mit ***doesn't* + Infinitiv**.

! Das **s** der 3. Person Singular steckt im Wort ***doesn't***:
*He/She/It **doesn't live** in Britain.*
(nicht: *He/She/It doesn't lives …*)

Verneinte Aussagen

Vergleiche:	Simple present	Simple past
	I **don't like** the Big Wheel.	I **didn't like** the Big Wheel.
	Sam **doesn't like** the Big Wheel.	Sam **didn't like** the Big Wheel.

---

d) *Yes/No* questions and short answers

Fragen

Vergleiche:	Simple present	Simple past
	Do you **like** the Big Wheel? – No, I **don't**.	**Did** you **like** the Big Wheel? – No, I **didn't**.
	Does Sam **like** the Big Wheel? – Yes, he **does**.	**Did** Sam **like** the Big Wheel? – Yes, he **did**.

Fragen im *simple present* bildest du

- bei *I, you, we, they* mit ***Do …***
- bei *he, she, it* mit ***Does …***

---

e) Questions with question words

*When **does** Abby **go** sailing? – On Sundays.*

*Why **does** Sam **have to** look after Lily in the afternoons?*
– Because his mum goes shopping then.

*When **do** lessons **finish** at your school?*

Fragen mit Fragewörtern *(When, Where, What, Why, How)* bildest du wie Entscheidungsfragen.
Das Fragewort steht am Anfang der Frage, vor *do* bzw. *does*.
Vergleiche:

	*She **goes** sailing.*
Entscheidungsfrage:	***Does** she **go** sailing?*
Frage mit Fragewort:	***When does** she **go** sailing?*

GF 3 Subject and object questions → *SB (p. 161)*

*What **happened** on Saturday morning?*
Was geschah am Samstagmorgen?

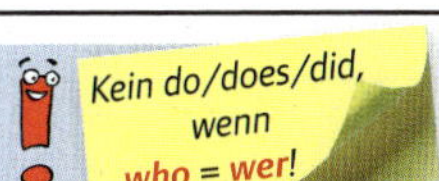

*Who **found** a note on the kitchen table? – Lucy.*
Wer fand eine Notiz auf dem Küchentisch? – …

*Who **invited** the Coopers to tea? – Mrs Pascoe.*
Wer hat die Coopers zum Tee eingeladen? – …

Subjektfragen sind „Wer oder was?"-Fragen.
Subjektfragen werden **ohne *do/does/did*** gebildet.
Die Wortstellung ist wie in Aussagesätzen, das Fragewort ist Subjekt des Fragesatzes. Vergleiche:

	Subjekt	Objekt
Aussage:	*Mrs Pascoe*	*invited the Coopers to tea.*
Subjektfrage:	*Who*	*invited the Coopers to tea?*
	Wer …?	Antwort: Mrs Pascoe

*What did Lucy **find** on the kitchen table?* – *A note.*
Was fand Lucy auf dem Küchentisch? – …

*Who did Lucy **call** on Saturday morning?* – *Her mum.*
Wen hat Lucy am Samstagmorgen angerufen? – …

*Who did Mrs Pascoe **invite** to tea?* – *The Coopers.*
Wen hat Mrs Pascoe zum Tee eingeladen? – …

*Who does Justin skype **with**?* – *His father.*
Mit wem skypt Justin? – …

Objektfragen sind „Wen/Wem oder was?"-Fragen.
Objektfragen werden im *simple present* **mit *do/does*** und im *simple past* **mit *did*** gebildet.
Das Fragewort ist Objekt des Fragesatzes.

	Objekt	Subjekt
Objektfrage:	***Who***	***did*** *Mrs Pascoe invite to tea?*
	Wen …?	Antwort: The Coopers

! Sieh dir den Beispielsatz und die Übersetzung gut an. Anders als im Deutschen steht die **Präposition** *(with)* in englischen Objektfragen am Ende der Frage.

GF 4 The present progressive ➜ SB (p. 162)

a) REVISION Simple present and present progressive

Simple present	*Morph often **plays** cards in the library.* Morph spielt oft Karten in der Bibliothek.
Present progressive	*Look, Morph **is playing** cards now.* Sieh mal, Morph spielt gerade Karten.

1 *Maya and Lucy are on Dartmoor. They**'re making** scones with Lucy's grandma.*
2 *Abby and Maya are by the sea. Skip **is running** along the beach.*

Mit dem *simple present* drückt man aus, dass etwas **wiederholt, regelmäßig, immer** oder **nie** geschieht (vgl. GF 2).

Mit dem *present progressive* drückt man aus, dass jemand **gerade dabei** ist, etwas zu tun, oder dass etwas **gerade im Gange** ist.

Das *present progressive* wird mit ***am/are/is* + *-ing*-Form** des Verbs gebildet: *I**'m playing** …/He**'s playing** …/ They**'re playing** …*

! Beachte folgende Besonderheiten:
1 Ein stummes **e** fällt weg: ***make*** ➜ ***making***, ***come*** ➜ ***coming***, ***dance*** ➜ ***dancing***
2 Nach einem einzelnen, betonten Vokal wird der Konsonant verdoppelt: ***run*** ➜ ***running***, ***get*** ➜ ***getting***, ***stop*** ➜ ***stopping***

b) The present progressive with future meaning

Maya: *Lucy **is joining** Plymstock's Gardening Club **next term**.*

Abby: *I**'m coming** home **in the next holidays**.*

Das *present progressive* wird auch verwendet, um über **feste Verabredungen** zu sprechen. Es muss aber deutlich sein, dass es sich um etwas Zukünftiges handelt, z. B. durch eine Zeitangabe *(tomorrow, next term, in the next holidays)* oder aus dem Zusammenhang.

GF 5 The *going to*-future ➜ SB (p. 163)

*Lucy **is going to sing** a Queen song at the audition today.*
Lucy wird beim heutigen Vorsingen einen *Queen*-Song singen.

*Leo's mum and dad **are going to be** at home this afternoon.*
Leos Mutter und Vater werden heute Nachmittag zu Hause sein.

Ich habe nicht vor, in einen neuen Klub einzutreten. …

Wenn du über **Absichten** und **Pläne** für die Zukunft sprechen willst, verwendest du das Futur mit ***going to***.

Es wird mit ***am/are/is going to* + Infinitiv** gebildet.
Die Kurzformen kennst du vom Verb ***be***:
I'm *going to*, ***you're*** *going to*, ***he's*** *going to* usw.

Die verneinten Formen kennst du ebenfalls schon:
I'm not *going to*, ***you aren't*** *going to*, ***he isn't*** *going to* usw.

Und auch Fragen und Kurzantworten sind wie beim Verb ***be***.

Das Futur mit *going to*

Bejahte Aussagen	Verneinte Aussagen	Fragen und Kurzantworten
I'm going to …	I'm not going to …	Are you going to watch the show?
You're going to …	You aren't going to …	– Yes, I am./No, I'm not.
He's/She's/It's going to …	He/She/It isn't going to …	Is he/she going to watch the show?
We're/You're/They're going to …	We/You/They aren't going to …	– Yes, he/she is./No, he/she isn't.

GF 6 The comparison of adjectives ➜ SB (pp. 164–165)

a) Comparison with *-er/-est*

*Julie is 13. Her brother Jake is **younger** – he's ten. Baby Jodie is the **youngest**, and James is the **oldest**.*

Die **Steigerungsformen** der Adjektive werden verwendet, um Dinge oder Personen miteinander zu vergleichen, z. B.:

young	***younger***	***(the) youngest***
jung	*jünger*	*am jüngsten; der/die/das jüngste …*
	↑ **Komparativ** *(comparative)*	↑ **Superlativ** *(superlative)*

Die Steigerung mit ***-er/-est*** verwendest du für
- **einsilbige** Adjektive *(young, long, nice, big, …)*
- **zweisilbige** Adjektive mit der **Endung *-y*** *(busy, easy, funny,).*

1 *James thinks that Jake is **nicer** than Julie.*
2 *The Millers' dog is **bigger** than Jodie.*
3 *The Millers' dog is the **happiest** dog in Britain.*

! Beachte folgende Besonderheiten:
1 Ein stummes ***e*** fällt weg: ***nice*** – ***nicer*** – ***nicest***
2 Nach einem einzelnen Vokal wird der Konsonant verdoppelt: ***big*** – ***bigger*** – ***biggest***
3 ***-y*** + ***-er/-est*** wird zu ***-ier/-iest***: ***happy*** – ***happier*** – ***happiest***

b) Comparison with *more/most*

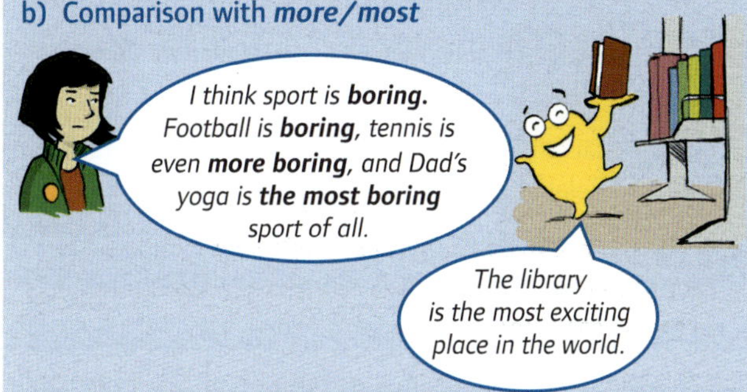

Die meisten anderen Adjektive werden mit ***more/most*** gesteigert:

boring	*langweilig*
more boring	*langweiliger*
(the) most boring	*am langweiligsten; der/die/das langweiligste …*

Weitere Beispiele:

beautiful	– *more beautiful*	– *(the) most beautiful*
careful	– *more careful*	– *(the) most careful*
expensive	– *more expensive*	– *(the) most expensive*

c) Irregular comparison

Die Steigerung der Adjektive

-er/-est	***more/most***	**unregelmäßig**
• Einsilbige Adjektive: *old* – *older* – *oldest*	Andere zweisilbige sowie *mehrsilbige Adjektive*	*good* – *better* – *best*
• Adjektive auf ***-y***: *happy* – *happier* – *happiest*	*exciting* – *more exciting* – *(the) most exciting*	*bad* – *worse* – *worst*
		much/many – *more* – *most*

d) *bigger than* – *as big as*

*The Millers' dog is **bigger than** Jodie.*
Der Hund der Millers ist größer als Jodie.

Wenn Personen oder Dinge **unterschiedlich** groß/alt/schnell/… sind, vergleichst du sie mit dem **Komparativ + *than*** (deutsch: „als"):

*I'm almost **as tall as** my mother now.*
Ich bin jetzt fast so groß wie meine Mutter.

Wenn Personen oder Dinge **gleich** groß/alt/schnell/… sind, vergleichst du sie mit ***as*** *big/old/fast/…* ***as***.

*My sister is 10. I'm **older than her**.*
Meine Schwester ist 10. Ich bin älter als sie.

! In Vergleichen mit ***than*** und ***as … as*** stehen die Personalpronomen ***me/him/her/us*** usw.

GF 7 Indirect speech ➜ SB (p. 166)

Direct speech

Lucy: ***"Grandma likes flowers."***
„Oma mag Blumen."

"Maya, you don't have to buy a present."
„Maya, du musst kein Geschenk kaufen."

In der **direkten Rede** (*direct speech*) gibt man wörtlich wieder, was jemand sagt oder schreibt (oder gesagt oder geschrieben hat).
Direkte Rede steht gewöhnlich in Anführungszeichen.

Indirect speech

Lucy ***says (that) her grandma likes flowers.***
Lucy sagt, dass ihre Oma Blumen mag.

Lucy ***says (that) Maya doesn't have to buy a present.***
Lucy sagt, dass Maya kein Geschenk kaufen muss.

Ella (zu Olivia): *"**I have** to help **my** mum."*
(Olivia berichtet:) *Ella says (that) **she has** to help **her** mum.*

In der **indirekten Rede** (*indirect speech* oder *reported speech*) berichtet man, was jemand sagt oder schreibt (oder gesagt oder geschrieben hat).
Die indirekte Rede wird mit Verben wie *say*, *tell sb.*, *add*, *answer*, *explain*, *write* eingeleitet.
Im Englischen steht vor der indirekten Rede **kein** Komma, und das Wort *that* („dass") wird oft weggelassen.

! Wie im Deutschen müssen in der indirekten Rede manchmal die Pronomen verändert werden. Dadurch kann sich auch die Verbform verändern (*"He, she, it – das **s** muss mit!"*).

GF 8 EXTRA Relative clauses ➔ SB (p. 167)

*I need one of those **things that look like a triangle**. For maths, you know. – Oh, you mean a **set square**.*
Ich brauche eins von diesen Dingern, die wie ein Dreieck aussehen. … – Oh, du meinst ein Geodreieck.

Relativsätze sind sehr nützlich, wenn du etwas beschreiben möchtest, wofür du das Wort nicht kennst oder wofür dir das Wort gerade nicht einfällt.

*There's **the little shop that makes its own chocolates**.*
… der kleine Laden, der seine eigenen Pralinen herstellt.

Relativsätze beschreiben genauer, über wen oder was man spricht:
Welcher Laden ist gemeint? – Der Laden, der seine eigenen Pralinen herstellt.

*Lucy is **the girl that wants to buy a set square**.*
Lucy ist das Mädchen, das ein Geodreieck kaufen will.

Welches Mädchen? – Das Mädchen, das ein Geodreieck kaufen will.

1 *I like **teachers that/who** laugh a lot.*
Ich mag Lehrer und Lehrerinnen, die viel lachen.

1 In Relativsätzen, die **Personen** beschreiben, kann statt ***that*** auch das Relativpronomen ***who*** stehen.

2 *The **shop that/which** sells expensive trainers is near the pedestrian zone.*
Der Laden, der teure Turnschuhe verkauft, …

2 In Relativsätzen, die **Dinge** (und Tiere) beschreiben, kann statt ***that*** auch das Relativpronomen ***which*** stehen.

*It's your grandma **that likes chocolates**, right?*
Es ist deine Oma, **die Pralinen mag**, richtig?

! Beachte die unterschiedliche **Wortstellung** im Englischen und im Deutschen.

GF 9 Adverbs of manner ➔ SB (p. 168)

a) Use

Adjectives *That's a **nice** idea.*
*Sam was very **excited**.*

Adverbs *"You do that Spiderman trick very **nicely**."*
*"Yes," Sam said **excitedly**.*
„Ja", sagte Sam aufgeregt/ mit aufgeregter Stimme.

Adjektive beziehen sich auf ein **Nomen**. Man verwendet sie, um Personen oder Dinge näher zu beschreiben – sie drücken aus, wie etwas oder jemand **ist**.
Adverbien der Art und Weise (*adverbs of manner*) beziehen sich auf ein **Verb**. Man verwendet sie, um Handlungen oder Vorgänge näher zu beschreiben – sie drücken aus, wie jemand etwas **tut** oder wie etwas **geschieht**.

Sam **schüttelte** langsam **den Kopf**.
*Sam **shook his head slowly**.*

! Im Deutschen können Adverbien der Art und Weise zwischen Verb und Objekt stehen. Englische *adverbs of manner* dürfen **nicht** zwischen Verb und Objekt stehen!

b) Regular forms

Adjective	***excited***	→	***excitedly***	**Adverb**
	nice	→	***nicely***	
	loud	→	***loudly***	

*Leo smiled **happily**.*
*It's not good to have a bath every day. We have to use water **responsibly**.* (verantwortungsvoll,-bewusst)
*Thank you very much. You did that job **fantastically**.*

Die meisten Adverbien der Art und Weise werden gebildet, indem *-ly* an das Adjektiv angehängt wird.

! Beachte folgende Besonderheiten:
1 *-y* + *-ly* wird zu *-ily*: ***happy*** → ***happily***
2 *-le* wird zu *-ly*: ***responsible*** → ***responsibly***
3 Nach *-ic* wird *-ally* angehängt: ***fantastic*** → ***fantastically***

Adverb *We ride our bikes **carefully**.* – Wir fahren **vorsichtig**.
Adjective *We're always **careful**.* – Wir sind immer **vorsichtig**.

Im Deutschen haben Adverbien der Art und Weise und Adjektive dieselbe Form, im Englischen in der Regel nicht.

c) Irregular forms

Sam is a ***good*** kung fu fighter. He fights ***well***.
*Rabbits are very **fast** animals. They can run very **fast**.*
*A job in a TV studio can be **hard** sometimes.*
*Justin's father often has to work very **hard**.*

Einige Adverbien der Art und Weise haben eine unregelmäßige Form, die du einzeln lernen musst:

Das Adverb zu ***good*** heißt ***well***.
Bei ***fast*** und ***hard*** haben Adjektiv und Adverb dieselbe Form.

GF 10 The present perfect ➜ *SB (pp. 169–171)*

a) Use

Grandma: *I've **made** some scones. I hope you're hungry.*
Ich habe Scones gemacht. …

Maya: *Yes, I am. I **haven't had** breakfast yet.*
… Ich habe noch nicht gefrühstückt.

Lucy: *Yes, Grandma, we've **checked** the times of the bus back to Plymouth. Don't worry.*
Ja, Oma, wir haben die Abfahrtszeiten des Busses … gecheckt. Mach dir keine Sorgen.

Mit dem *present perfect* drückt man aus, dass jemand irgendwann etwas getan hat oder dass irgendwann etwas geschehen ist. Es ist nicht wichtig, wann das war – deshalb wird auch kein genauer Zeitpunkt genannt.

Oft hat die Handlung **Auswirkungen** auf die Gegenwart oder die Zukunft: Lucy hat die Abfahrtszeiten des Busses nachgesehen, sodass ihre Oma sich nun keine Sorgen machen muss.

(Zum Unterschied zwischen *present perfect* und *simple past* vgl. GF 11).

b) Form: the past participle

Das *present perfect* wird mit ***have/has*** und der 3. Form des Verbs gebildet.
Die 3. Form heißt **Partizip Perfekt (*past participle*)**.

1 *We've **checked** the times of the bus.*
*I've **texted** you the time that we arrive.*
*Sam **hasn't finished** his bath yet.*
*Don't open the door. The bus **hasn't stopped** yet.*
*Maya, **have** you **tried** Grandma's scones?*

1 Bei **regelmäßigen Verben** hängst du ***-ed*** an den Infinitiv, um das *past participle* zu bilden:
check + ed → ***checked*** • ***text + ed*** → ***texted***
Beachte die Besonderheiten der Schreibung und der Aussprache. (Vgl. GF 1a)

2 *I **haven't eaten** anything today.*
*Oh no, Sam **has fallen** in the mud.*
*I've never **been** on a tractor before.*

2 **Unregelmäßige Verben** (SB, S. 248–249) haben eigene Formen: *(to)* ***eat, ate, eaten***
Die 2. Form ist die *simple past*-Form *(ate)*.
Die 3. Form ist das *past participle (eaten)*.

c) Positive and negative statements

Das *present perfect*

Bejahte Aussagen	Verneinte Aussagen	Langformen
I've fallen …	I haven't finished …	I/You/We/They have (not) fallen …
You've fallen …	You haven't finished …	
He's/She's/It's fallen …	He/She/It hasn't finished …	He/She/It has (not) fallen …
We've/You've/They've fallen …	We/You/They haven't finished …	

! Das *present perfect* wird immer mit ***have/has*** gebildet, egal ob im Deutschen „haben" oder „sein" steht.

d) Questions and short answers

***Has** you ever **tried** sheep's milk?*
*– Yes, I **have**./No, I **haven't**.*
***Has** the rain **stopped** yet?*
*– Yes, it **has**./No, it **hasn't**.*
***What have** you **done**, Maya?*

In Fragen sind **Subjekt** und ***have/has*** vertauscht.
Fragewörter stehen wie immer am Satzanfang.
! Im *present perfect* gibt es **keine Fragen mit *when***.
When fragt nach einem Zeitpunkt – und dafür musst du das *simple past* verwenden.

e) The present perfect with adverbs of indefinite time

*I'm not hungry. **I've already eaten**.*
Ich habe schon gegessen.

*I've **seen** the film **before**. I don't want to watch it again.*
***Have** you **ever been** to Paris? – No, **I've never been** to Paris. But **I've always wanted** to go there.*

***Have** you **done** your homework **yet**?*
*Where are Emily and Olivia? – **I've just seen** Emily in the garden. But Olivia **hasn't arrived yet**.*

Das *present perfect* drückt aus, dass etwas **irgendwann** geschehen ist. Daher stehen keine genauen Zeitangaben in *present perfect*-Sätzen. Aber das *present perfect* wird oft mit **unbestimmten Zeitangaben** verwendet:
already *schon, bereits;* ***always*** *(schon) immer;*
before *(vorher) schon mal;* ***just*** *gerade (eben), soeben;*
never *(noch) nie;* ***not … yet*** *noch nicht;* ***often*** *(schon) oft*

Und in Fragen findest du oft:
ever? *jemals?/schon mal?;* ***yet?*** *schon?*

! Diese Adverbien stehen direkt vor dem Verb.
Ausnahmen: ***before*** und ***yet*** stehen am Satzende.

GF 11 EXTRA Present perfect or simple past? ➜ SB (p. 171)

Son: *I've **checked** your computer, Mum. It's OK now.*

Mum: *Thank you. **When did** you **do** it?*

Son: *I **checked** it **last night** when you were in bed.*

***Has** Grandma **phoned** **yet**? –*
*Yes, she **phoned** **ten minutes ago**. Everything's fine.*

Present perfect:
– wenn du sagen willst, **dass etwas (irgendwann) geschehen ist**
– wenn du fragen willst, **ob etwas geschehen ist**
Ein Zeitpunkt wird nicht genannt. Aber in *present perfect*-Sätzen stehen oft unbestimmte Zeitangaben wie *already, before, ever, just, never, not … yet, often, yet*.

Simple past:
– wenn du sagen oder fragen willst, **wann etwas geschehen ist**
In *simple past*-Sätzen stehen oft genaue Zeitangaben wie *yesterday, last year, an hour ago, in 2012*.

GF 12 *some* and *any* and their compounds ➜ SB (p. 172)

a) some/any

\+ *I've made **some biscuits**. And there's **some milk** too.*
… ein paar Kekse … … etwas Milch …

some steht vor allem in **bejahten** Aussagesätzen (+).
Es bedeutet „einige, ein paar" *(some scones/CDs/boys/…)* oder „etwas" *(some milk/money/music/…)*.

– *I **can't** see **any sheep**. And there **aren't any cows**.*
… keine Schafe … … keine Kühe …

any steht vor allem in **verneinten** Aussagesätzen (–) und in **Fragen** (?).

? *Are there **any scones**?*
Gibt es Scones?
*Do you have **any questions**?*
Habt ihr (irgendwelche) Fragen?

! Im Deutschen kann man fragen „Gibt es Scones?", aber im Englischen steht meist *any*: *Are there any scones?*

b) somebody/anybody – something/anything

+	*I think there's **someone** at the door.*	jemand
–	*No, there **isn't anybody** there.*	niemand
?	*Can you see **anyone**?*	(irgend)jemand
+	*Let's go and get **something** to eat.*	etwas
–	*I'm too nervous. I **can't** eat **anything**.*	nichts
?	*Is there **anything** I can do for you?*	(irgend)etwas

Für die **Zusammensetzungen** mit **some** *(somebody/someone, something)* und **any** *(anybody/anyone, anything)* gelten dieselben Regeln.

c) Offers and requests

! In Fragen, mit denen man etwas **anbietet** oder um etwas **bittet**, verwendet man *some, somebody/someone, something*.

GF 13 The *will*-future ➔ SB (p. 173)

a) Use

*Next Saturday, you**'ll see** some tricks that I've never done before.*
Nächsten Samstag werden Sie Kunststücke sehen, …

*When **will** the rehearsal **be** over? – Not till three.*
Wann wird die Probe vorbei sein? – Nicht vor drei.

*Maya probably **won't come** without Lucy.*
Maya wird wahrscheinlich nicht ohne Lucy kommen.

*It **will be** warm and sunny tomorrow.*
Morgen wird es warm und sonnig (sein/werden).

*Hurry, or we**'ll miss** the girls.*
Beeil dich, sonst **verpassen** wir die Mädchen.

Du verwendest das **Futur mit *will***, um zu sagen, was in der Zukunft geschehen wird.
Das *will-future* steht oft mit Zeitangaben wie *tomorrow, next Saturday, soon, in a few weeks*.

Wenn **Vermutungen** geäußert werden, steht häufig *I (don't) think, I'm (not) sure, maybe* oder *probably*.

Oft geht es um Dinge, die man nicht beeinflussen kann, z. B. **Vorhersagen** über das Wetter.

Im Deutschen benutzen wir oft das Präsens, wenn wir Vermutungen äußern oder Vorhersagen machen.
Im Englischen steht das *will-future*.

! **Vorsicht** – wenn du über **Pläne** für die Zukunft sprichst, verwendest du *going to*, nicht *will*.
(Zum *going to-future* vgl. GF 5)

b) Form

*Spain **will be** warm and sunny in June.*
*I'm sure you**'ll like** it.*

*They're a very good team. I think they**'ll win**.*

***Will** I **meet** Stella at your party on Friday?*
*– No, you **won't**. She **won't be** in Plymouth on Friday.*

What **will** the weather ***be*** like at the weekend?

My sister ***wants to*** help us. … ***möchte/will*** uns helfen.
My sister ***will*** help us. … ***wird*** uns helfen.

Das *will-future* besteht aus ***will* + Infinitiv**.
Es gibt für alle Personen nur eine Form.

Die **Kurzform** von *will* ist *'ll*: *I'll, you'll, he'll, she'll* usw.

Die **verneinte Form** von *will* heißt ***won't***
(Langform: *will not*).

! **Nicht verwechseln:**
- ***I want to do*** heißt „ich will tun", „ich möchte tun".
- ***I will do*** heißt „ich werde tun".

Das Futur mit *will*

Bejahte Aussagen	Verneinte Aussagen	Fragen
I'll/You'll/He'll/She'll/It'll go	I/You/He/She/It won't stay	Will you/he/she/it/they go?
We'll/You'll/They'll go	We/You/They won't stay	– Yes, I/he/she/it/they will./ No, I/he/she/it/they won't.

GF 14 EXTRA Question tags ➔ SB (p. 174)

a) Use

*It's a lovely day, **isn't it?***
Schöner Tag, nicht wahr?

*But we can play frisbee on our own, **can't we?***
Aber wir können ja allein Frisbee spielen, nicht?

Du kennst bereits das englische Frageanhängsel *right?*: *You're Amy, right?* – „Du bist Amy, nicht wahr?"

In den Beispielen links findest du weitere Frageanhängsel. Frageanhängsel werden häufig in der gesprochenen Sprache verwendet.

b) Form

bejaht	verneint
*The bus stop **is** near here,*	***isn't it?***
*I **can go** by bike,*	***can't I?***
*The show **was** great,*	***wasn't it?***
*We **saw** lots of street artists,*	***didn't we?***

Die Frageanhängsel bestehen aus **Hilfsverb** *(is, are, can, do, …)* + **Personalpronomen** *(I, you, she, we, …)*.
Wenn der Aussagesatz bejaht ist, ist das Frageanhängsel verneint.

verneint	bejaht
*The show **isn't** over now,*	***is it?***
*He **can't speak** Chinese,*	***can he?***
*The tickets **weren't** too expensive,*	***were they?***
*They **don't have** Carnival in England,*	***do they?***

Wenn der Aussagesatz verneint ist, ist das Frageanhängsel bejaht.

Checkpoint 2

1 WORDS Free time

1 sunglasses 2 show, town hall 3 theatre, play 4 concert
5 earphones 6 nervous, auditions, stage

2 Lunchtime

you're going to sing is going to dance are you going to play
aren't going to play is going to be Are you going to come

3 An email

1 bigger than Plymouth 2 as quiet as Plymouth
3 more expensive than Plymouth 4 as exciting as the sea
5 sunnier and windier than London

4 Where are they?

1 B 2 C

5 After school

a) C b) 1 R 2 W 3 R 4 W 5 R 6 W 7 R 8 W 9 W 10 R

Checkpoint 3

1 PRONUNCIATION Silent letters

a) 1 straight on 2 theatre 3 chocolates 4 juice 5 souvenirs 6 whisper

2 WORDS Nina in town

a) 1 a tin of soup 2 a bottle of orange juice 3 a box of chocolates
b) 1 pedestrian zone 2 post office 3 shopping centre

3 Master Wu and the magic book

1 Justin says the boat is old and broken. 2 Leo says he can do that.
3 Sam says he can't feel his legs. 4 Maya says she's going in.

4 In a sports shop

Lösungsvorschlag:
- I'd like some tennis balls, please.
- Eight, please. How much do they cost?
- Oh, that's too much. Do you have cheaper balls?
- Yes, that's OK. Can I have two tins of four, please?
- What colours are there?/What colours do you have?
- I like orange/green/yellow. I'd like orange/..., please.
- Here you are.

5 Telling someone the way

a) **Lösungsvorschlag:** Go along Plym Road and at the café on the corner turn right into Duke Street. Then turn left into Church Road. Go straight on past the church and turn right into New Street. Cross the road and the phone shop is on the left.

b) **Lösungsvorschlag:** Go along Old Road and turn left into Church Road. Turn right into New Street. Opposite the church there's a sandwich shop. Turn right past the sandwich shop. The souvenir shop is next to the sandwich shop.

6 Where you live

a) **Lösungsvorschlag:** I live in ... It's a big town/city/small town/village near ... in Germany. There's a shopping centre/some cafés/ ... (I think) Plymouth is bigger/smaller than ... There's an old part of town with old houses, a museum,... There isn't a harbour but there's a river with ... We don't have a hill like the Hoe, but there's a nice lake.

b) **Lösungsvorschlag:**
- No, I don't. The coast is about ... kilometres away./Yes, I do. There's a big harbour and a beach.
- Yes, we have a new sports centre./No, there isn't a sports centre, but there's a swimming pool, a football club and a tennis club.
- Yes, we have two shopping centres./No, there isn't, but there are lots of shops in the next town.
- No, there aren't any farms./Yes, there's a farm not far away.
- In my free time I go to the shops or the park with friends.
- Yes, there's a café with great ice cream.

Checkpoint 4

1 WORDS On the moor

1 countryside 2 fields, grass, sheep, cows, valleys
3 dirty, mud, bath 4 sweet lambs, barn, strong, missing
5 adventure, heavy, mugs, cocoa

2 Nina has been there

Have you ever been I've stayed Have you ever seen
I've never visited

3 Let's find it

letterboxing

4 Buckfast otters and butterflies

b) 1 R 2 W 3 R 4 W 5 N 6 W 7 N 8 R

c) **Lösungsvorschlag:**
1 British otters; British otters are shy and they like to live alone.
2 feeding time; The last feeding time is at 4:30 pm.
3 'Otter experience'; At the 'Otter experience' you can find out more about the otters and their keepers.
4 When; You can see the otters from 10:00 am to 5:00 pm in summer.

Checkpoint 5

1 WORDS UK festivals

1 candles 2 put on, costumes, paint 3 raise, charity
4 take part, parade 5 crowds, celebrate, fireworks

2 I don't think I'll go to the parade

2 I don't think I'll finish this christmas cake.
3 I think I'll have an apple.
4 I think I'll go too.

3 Christmas in the UK

1 Früchtekuchen, Marzipanüberzug, Zuckerguss, dekoriert
2 am Morgen des ersten Weihnachtstages 3 ein Knallbonbon mit einem Papierhut, einem kleinen Plastikspielzeug und einem Witz darin
4 Truthahn, Röstkartoffeln, Gemüse, Früchtekuchen mit Soße
5 Fernsehen: 15 Uhr Weihnachtsansprache der Königin, oft Zirkusvorstellung, dann Tee mit Weihnachtskuchen, mit Geschenken spielen

4 A German celebration

1 In spring and summer every year. 2 There are over two million visitors. 3 Yes, she/he will take part in the children's parade, wear a costume and play the big drum in a band. 4 There are cool rides, a big wheel, a ghost train, souvenir stalls, and 'Losbuden' – stalls where you buy tickets and maybe win a prize. 5 Yes, there will be lots of food and stalls, snacks and ice cream. 6 There are clowns, jugglers and 'Wurfspiele' – games where you throw balls and maybe win a prize.

Checkpoint 6

1 WORDS What's missing?

a) guide Prince built guards defended enter enemies
b) cold/cough cough/cold headache sore throat temperature thermometer

2 Sam's dream

am walking sew is riding are standing point am are wearing
am wearing are fighting is making run

3 Two reports

Report A: 6, 3, 5 **Report B:** 2, 4, 1

4 A great trip

Beachte: Einleitung, Hauptteil, Schluss. W-Fragen beantworten. Abschnitte im Hauptteil: *First, Next, After lunch, ...* Im *simple past* schreiben. Adjektive und Adverbien verwenden. Mit einem Schlusssatz abrunden.